Dandelions & Snails

A Journey From the Dark Days of War, to the Golden
Fields of Peace

A True Story

by

A.C. Miles-Smith

To
Sue and Jon
with Best
wishes

Anna.

Published by A.C. Miles-Smith

For more copies of this book please email:

ac_miles_smith@outlook.com

ISBN: 978-0-9932646-0-3

CONTENTS

ACROSS THE FIELDS

Sweetness
came to me
across the fields
up from the sea
it spoke of
childhood days
and blossoms
on the tree

When Jesus was a little boy
he too played
in the fields
he broke a branch
from the hawthorn tree
he ripped
his gown
on thorns
he should have stayed
he would have been
safe
in Cornish arms

Sweetness
came to me today
it spoke
of childhood days
it kissed
the cobwebs
in the barn
and spoke
in whispering
phrase

it spoke
of childhood days
with voices
from the past
it flew around
the old churchyard
it shook
the swaying mast
with a skip
and a hop
it then was gone
to where
I never asked.

John, Susan and Anna on the standing stone, first field

PROLOGUE

I return to the place of my birth. As expected everything has changed. The tiny cottage where I, and my brother and sisters were born, has now been renovated. Life has moved on. All that remains are the ghosts of the past. Yet the spirits whisper through the birds, the grass the flowers and the granite, they tell me to capture those golden memories and take them to that place where they can never be forgotten.

So armed with my note book and my pen, I began to write the story of my childhood and the poems of my dreams.

Dandelions grew all around the cottage door. God gave them simplicity and made them humble and bright. Outside the cottage, in the fields and in the lanes there were always snails for me to eat. The hedge that ran down from the cottage to the fields was covered with snails.

My earliest memories are of picking the snails off the hedge, I thought they were humbugs. Then I would cram as many as I could into my mouth and toddle as fast as my fat legs could carry me. I knew that my mother, keeping a constant vigil through the tiny granite widow which looked down the lane, would see me and give chase. I then had a few minutes to crunch as many as I could and swallow, before she reached me and tried to extract the remains of the poor creatures.

And so on my return to the cottage, I stood there in a trance, the threads of my book started to appear from the ether, and the world stopped turning. The fir tree that my father had planted in the garden, when my brother John was born, had now grown into a tree of great strength and stature, of about fifty feet high. The small bedroom window in which I would sit to write poems, was now like a fairy tale turret.

The cows in the field stood perfectly still and the sun, low in the autumn afternoon sky was just a big bowl of warm orange custard, that you could touch with your fingers if you leant forward across the field. In this magnified silence, the ivy grew in reverent greenness around the granite cottage and barn. I had a wonderful feeling that I was a spirit, caught like a time traveller in a vortex. I was able to experience through a portal of time the voices of the ghosts and spirits of the past. Not just the voices but also the meanings: the purpose of the granite and the ivy, and I was at one with the beauty of my surroundings.

I listened to what those spirits whispered. They talked through the birds, the grass, the flowers and the granite and they took me back, down the years to my childhood.

The pieces of the jigsaw started to collect in my mind and I knew I must tell my story. The story that starts before the Second World War in Edgeley Stockport and concludes in Cornwall in the aftermath of the war, when England became a huge dice in the hands of peace, being shaken, ready to be thrown, and a new number to be called.

In the cities they had suffered terribly during the war, in Manchester, Coventry, Leeds, Plymouth and Liverpool. Also in the German cities, as in Berlin and Nuremberg, there was great devastation. .

And for a time in this aftermath the members of the human race were kinder and more considerate to each other. They remembered the pain and realized how fragile the human entity is.

My parents Arthur Slater and Marjorie Smith were born in Edgeley, Stockport, just before the Second World War. They were married in Stockport. They later moved to North Wales, where Arthur, being a conscientious objector, went to work on the Forestry Commission, and also to look after Italian prisoners of war. From Wales my parents moved down to Lamorna in Cornwall, where an artists' colony was evolving. From Lamorna my parents moved to Boswarthen near Madron, and that's where I came in.

I will now start to weave in as much detail as I can, the intricate tapestry of the story of my grandparents, and the events which led my parents to embrace the wild bohemian lifestyle which they embarked upon. My first stitches are those of the pre-war years.

*This picture was taken at Gawsworth house in Abergele,
North Wales in the late 1930's*

9

The photograph on the previous page portrays an idyllic lifestyle. This picture was taken at Gawsworth house in Abergele, North Wales in the late 1930's. This was known as a 'Friends Meeting House', which was a meeting house for members of the Quaker Religion, and all who might be interested in their philosophies. They were all pacifists who did not believe in war and killing their fellow men. The large lady on the front left of the photograph was my grandmother Edith Slater and the man next to her on the left was my granddad Hampson Slater. Next to him was Edith's brother, and next to him wearing his jaunty hat was Jim Slater, Edith and Hampson's son who was drowned at sea during the war. Around the table there are then more friends until we come to Arthur Slater, the blonde man leaning forward on the table. He was Edith and Hampson's eldest son and Jim's only sibling. Next to Arthur sits my mother Marjorie Smith. And this is where Marjorie and Arthur first met and fell in love. My mother is dressed in the spirit of the thirties with the elegant handbag and her dress made by the family's tailoress, a lovely lady called Bessie Bleazby. Bessie made all Marjorie's clothes, and dresses and suits for Marjorie's mother and father, Emily and Miles. They were all good people and now are all gone.

For the privileged in the 1930's, there were still the luxuries which had been established in the heady days of the twenties. There was high fashion and supreme art deco creations in every sphere. There was inspirational music. There were the soft romantic ballads such as "These Foolish Things" and "I'll be Seeing You", sung by men with deep, mellow, well spoken voices, and women with voices of velvet clarity. These were often accompanied by gentle tones of the double bass and cello.

Time was on the side of those lucky ones who could dress in Haute Couture, eat at the finest restaurants and dance to the sound of the loud and happy big bands playing at the cabarets and music halls. They were blissfully unaware of the political situation of the time.

Underneath this ostentatious veneer was the creeping flip side of the thirties. In the gathering depression of this decade there was high unemployment, in fact the figure reached three million. Families did their best to survive but hunger was creeping in. The dole was not enough to live on. The government propaganda machine portrayed the jobless families as lazy. The truth was there were no jobs. Men wanted to work. They did not want to see their families starve.

Consequently hunger marches were organized. Men marched to London from all over the country, and from as far as Scotland, to let their plight be known. Some of these men had fought in the First World War, fought for their country, and now they suffered the indignity of hunger through no fault of their own. Was this poverty and hunger the result of the government gearing up for war again? Were they draining revenue from the poor to buy armaments? No one knew. No one wanted war. Yet the pre-war propaganda machine of the late 1930's in England chose to keep the public in ignorance of the developing conflicts in Europe, and the potential threat of war. The signing of the Treaty of Versailles in June of 1919, that post World War One document which had ordered Germany to disarm, and swear an oath that the countries would never go to war with each other again, was still inherent in the psyche of both English and German nations.

The majority of the English people were unaware that Germany was rearming. Still as late as 1938 when Neville Chamberlain visited Hitler, there was a naive trusting Britishness which pervaded the thoughts of the English, leading them to believe that war could be avoided.

Hitler had other ideas on his mind. The Englishman who had come to tea with him was polite, courteous and obsequious. From this meeting, Chamberlain assumed that he had secured peace, whilst Hitler assumed that the English were worms which he could easily crush without resistance.

Hitler had no intention of honouring the promise he had signed.

On September 1st 1939, Hitler invaded Poland, and in defence of Poland, Great Britain declared war on Germany on 3rd September 1939. Now a coalition government was formed in England with Mr. Winston Churchill as First Lord of the Admiralty. He was made Prime Minister in 1940. Now with a strong leader the British were given the courage they needed to withstand the onslaught.

And in that deep, forceful, spirited voice that seemed to be carving the words in stone, Churchill broadcast to his nation:

* "We shall fight on the beaches, in the fields, in the streets, and in the hills –we shall never surrender".

* Reproduced with permission of Curtis Brown, London on behalf of the Estate of Winston S. Churchill.

Copyright © The Estate of Winston S. Churchill

Barbara Lawry Boase, a Cornish born girl can remember the morning that war was declared in Britain. She was standing in her father's bedroom when the announcement came over the Pye radio. Barbara was twelve years old and they had just taken over the farm at Kenidjack. Even though her father was very ill, he said as soon as he was fit enough he would sign up again. During the First World War her father, William Samson, had fought in Flanders. After the Battle of the Somme he worked for thirty six hours, without a break, to help carry the dead, through the mud of the trenches. Tragically, just three weeks after they moved to the farm, Barbara's father died and Barbara and her mother had to carry on alone.

Some nights Barbara cried herself to sleep because the work was that hard. Several years later Barbara was on an European trip. She heard the coach driver announce 'We are now approaching Flanders', and she felt as if a knife had gone through her heart. Her father had promised that if he became well enough again he would return to Flanders to pay his last respects to his dead comrades. Barbara took solace from the fact that she had been chosen to make that journey for him.

From the loss of all those lives the world should have gained some wisdom. Yet on that bleak September day in 1939 the stage was set, once again, to re-enact the very same scenario.

It was not until the early part of 1940, that the aerial bombing of British towns and cities began. Across England the German bombers flew to annihilate the towns, the lives and the souls of those with enough audacity to stand against the mighty 'Fuhrer.' And in the hitherto sleepy suburb of Edgeley in the town of Stockport in the city of Manchester, blackouts were enforced and families fled to their bunkers and cellars to shelter. And that is where the story of my family begins.

I: 191 OLD CHAPEL STREET, EDGELEY, STOCKPORT 1940

Beth and Jim are in love, true love. When the sirens wail and the scramble for survival begins, Jim's mother Edith, his father Hampson, his brother Arthur, and also his aunt Cissy all run down to the cellar, under the living room for shelter.

Beth and Jim don't want to go down to the cellar, and against his mother's wishes Jim hides with Beth under the heavy oak table in the living room. The bombs drop all around. How could they have known then that they did not have long to be together, that their lives were suspended on fine threads? They were soon to be married. Jim was Arthur's brother. Had he survived, he would have been my Uncle. He was killed in naval action, as his returning convoy bringing food to England was bombed. Edith and Hampson were my grandma and grandad.

The houses in Edgeley, Stockport were all built with cellars approximately five and a half feet high and it was here at 191

Old Chapel Street, that they made their cellar into an air raid shelter.

Underneath them in the cellar, the rest of the family try to keep their spirits strong. There are basic provisions in the cellar and a radio. There is a special cupboard with a wire mesh front to keep what little food they have fresh. In the cellar are beds, buckets and candles. Aunty Cissy wears an old leather coat which creaks every time she moves. They huddle together for warmth and comfort. They play cards, tell stories and pray. All the while they listen to the radio. Lord Haw Haw transmits from Germany and tries to break their spirits. My family just laugh at him, they are of the Quaker religion and have strong faith.

Above the rooftops of the houses in Edgeley, the German bombers fly over.

The streets are dark and blacked out, there are no lights to be seen. The noise of the bombers is loud above in the night sky. The roulette game continues, and every minute seems to take an hour. Beth and Jim kiss under the heavy oak table.

"Don't be afraid" says Jim to Beth

"Our love is too strong for anyone or anything to take that away from us".

Then the all clear sounds and they realize they have been saved again. Gradually everyone returns upstairs to the living room. Edith peeps through the blackout curtain and looks down the street. Fires are burning all around them. A house nearby has been completely demolished. The bricks are still tumbling to the floor as if in slow motion. There is no sign of the family, yet all their possessions and furniture are exposed. The table is still intact and is laid for supper. The family cat wanders nonchalantly out from under the table and tiptoes gracefully around the smoking rubble, like a willowy ballerina. High above from the night sky, the stars and moon shine down on the chesterfield settee and the velvet cushions. A soft rain starts to descend.

Jim decides he wants to join the Navy. He wants to play his part, to help provide for and protect his family and his country. He can no longer see this devastation take place night after night. He wants to put an end to it all. This decision is painful for Edith and Hampson as they have campaigned all their lives for pacifism, and attended Quaker meetings in an attempt to bring peace into the world. The Society of Friends, whom were generally called Quakers, make no show of their religion. The movement was started by George Fox who was born in 1624. The Quakers believe in a quiet inward religion akin to Buddhism. They believe in the patient endurance of other men's violence. However they respect their son and the choice he has made. Jim makes a concession for his parents. He joins the Merchant Navy, so that he will be able to bring in food and clothing for the nation.

Beth is very distressed, but nothing can change Jim's mind. Jim must do what he feels is right, and he joins the navy.

Jim's brother Arthur adopts the opposing philosophy, he refuses to fight or have any part in the action, and, going against all public opinion he becomes a conscientious objector. Arthur was two years older than Jim. He had had more time to assimilate his parents' religion. It was at the Quaker meetings that the young Arthur had listened to and digested his parents' pacifist philosophies. Arthur was not a coward. He would stand up to any man in hand to hand combat, but he would not go to war. Arthur is adamant that he will not kill another man. Such non-conformists were ostracized from their community and were said to bring shame and disgrace on their families. White feathers were posted through their doors.

The conscientious objectors were well educated men. They read psychology and philosophy and were inspired by the radical texts of Marx, Engels and Jung. They tried to convey the futility of a planet at war with its own inhabitants. They also wanted to expose the cruel machinations of war. But it was too little, too late. As Winston Churchill said in his diary entitled 'The Gathering Storm':

* "The English people through their un-wisdom, had allowed the evil to re-arm".

Aldous Huxley in his book of 1938 entitled 'Ends and Means' writes that

** "Every road towards a better state of society is blocked, sooner or later, by war, by threats of war, by preparations for war". Aldous then continues

"All the governments are actively engaged in making a subtle kind of propaganda that is directed against potential enemies, but not against war, and that they proclaim the necessity of piling up enormous armaments for the purpose

* Reproduced with permission of Curtis Brown, London on behalf of the Estate of Winston S. Churchill Copyright © The Estate of Winston S. Churchill

** ENDS AND MEANS by Aldous Huxley. Copyright © 1938 by Aldous Huxley. Reprinted by permission of Georges Borchardt, Inc., for the Estate of Aldous Huxley.

of counter-attack and retaliation, and they actually build those armaments to the tune, in most European countries, of nearly or fully half the total national revenue".

Still today the war machine trundles on, making money and profit from horror and misery.

And so a dichotomy arises in the family, each brother doing what he believes to be right. Jim facing the German enemy, Arthur facing the hidden enemy: the eternal war machine. And who can say who is wrong and who is right? Men and women down through the ages have had to face similar dilemmas of individual conscience, where the ultimate decision can only come from their heart alone.

In William Shakespeare's, 'Hamlet, Prince of Denmark,' Hamlet has to make a similar decision of the heart. In Act III, scene I Hamlet is driven to contemplate suicide by the ghostly revelation that his father has been murdered by his uncle, who then proceeded to seduce his mother.

He wrestles with his conscience

" To be or not to be, - that is the question: -
Whether 'tis nobler in the mind to suffer
The slings and arrows of outrageous fortune,
Or to take arms against a sea of troubles,
And by opposing end them? "

Eventually, it is the fear of the unknown in the after-life which prevents Hamlet from taking his own life. Arthur and Jim both had to wrestle with their own hearts and consciences. Arthur had made his decision. He knew in his heart that he was strong enough to withstand the contemptuous derision of the masses.

19

The conscientious objectors were not cowards. They did have to suffer the slings and arrows of public outrage.

Arthur and his brother Jim, were so different in their attitudes. Jim felt the need to act, to tend to the immediate needs of his family and his country. Arthur took a longer view of the situation. He could only see the futility of war, and the endless mindless suffering of the human race.

He read the works of the poets and the philosophers: Siegfried Sassoon, Rupert Brooke, Wilfred Owen, T.S. Eliot, John Keats, W.B. Yeats, Robert Burns, Aldous Huxley and George Orwell. He listened to the age old voices of wisdom, that for so long down through the ages have tried to steer the human race to safety through their religions. He read the philosophies of the Quakers, the Buddhists and the Christians.

Dialogue of the Brothers

Jim - "Move and step with the tide, to stop the killing and the genocide"

Arthur - "Hatred can never bring peace, only compassion can bring release"

Jim - "But we must act, protect our land, face the foe, and make a stand"

Arthur - "The human race is cruel and unkind, and the only species to wage war on its own kind"

Jim - "No we must fight to protect our land, fight if necessary hand to hand."

Brothers in arms: Arthur and Jim

Duty of the Heart

And so the brothers must depart
Each to do the duty
Of his own heart
One to fight the war
With swords
One to fight the war
With words
Was it easier to go
With the masses and fight
Or stand alone
And be condemned
For what you thought
Was right?

A.C. Miles-Smith

When Jim leaves his home for the last time it is a sad day. Jim kisses his mum, Edith and his dad, Hampson, goodbye. He is dressed in his Naval uniform. He wears his white and blue cap and his square white shoulder cape.

His mum and dad are proud of him. And he looks so handsome. Arthur hugs his brother and says goodbye, although they had conflicting ideas, the brothers would not let this destroy their love for each other and for the family.

Outside the house in Edgeley there is a long straight street of about one mile in length. This leads to Stockport Station where Jim must board his train which will take him to

Liverpool and his waiting ship. Edith watches as Jim closes the garden gate. He sets off down the long, straight road to the station. On either side of him are the red brick houses of his youth with their smoking winter chimneys giving forth their nightly smog, in a dark security blanket of the Industrial North. On either side of him he hears the cry of the rag and bone man, "Rag Bone, Rag Bone" he cries as he rides his pony and cart around the streets. The women would exchange their old clothes for a donkey stone, so called because it was made in Blackpool with cement and sand. With this they would clean their front door steps, while the children would play with the balloons the rag bone man had tied to his trap. Jim leaves behind these warm kind hearts of his childhood days. On either side are the cobbled alley ways where the brothers played, in their laced up boots and their woolly hats.

Jim and Arthur's mum, Edith, knitted all their hats and jumpers. She knitted for the community, for anyone having a baby, for children in Africa and anyone in need. If you stood long enough in Edith's living room you would find yourself in a woolly hat and gloves.

Edith had worked in the cotton mill from the age of ten. She had worked from six o'clock in the morning until six o'clock at night, for six pence a week. The lantern men from the mills would patrol the streets in the morning, to knock on the bedroom windows with their long white poles, making sure the children were awake and getting ready for work. If Edith was given an apple to eat on her way to the mill, she would often hear the patter of bare feet behind her on the cobbles and a child's voice cry "Corkers corkers". Then Edith would save her half eaten apple for the little child.

Edith often had no shoes to wear. Yet she would say "I grumbled because I had no shoes, until I met a man with no feet". Edith was very wise and another one of her favorite sayings was:

* "The rain it raineth on the just
And also on the unjust fella;
But chiefly on the just
Because
The unjust steals
The just's
Umbrella"

Later on in life Edith would attend 'Ban the Bomb' marches. Because she was a rather large lady she took great delight in sitting in the middle of the road and waiting for a police officer to come to lift her away. She had a good sense of humour. She knew it would take more than one man to move her. It actually took four. They would be very polite and, restoring her back to the pavement would ask her if she was alright. As soon as they were out of sight she would go and sit in the road again.

Now her son, Jim, is going to make the world a better place for his mum, his dad, his girl and brother. Edith climbs onto a chair to peer through the front room window and watches him as far as she can. Jim keeps turning to wave. Eventually all she can see of him is his white collar, bobbing like a small white butterfly in the distance. And then he is gone.

The family never see Jim again. Several months after Jim's departure a telegram arrives at the house. On its' return from the Atlantic, bringing food from America Jim's ship has been

*Quote by Charles Synge Christopher Bowen.

torpedoed and sunk, there has been heavy losses of life and Jim is missing.

Edith is in great shock and tells everyone that Jim had been the best swimmer in the school. Hampson suffers silently. At the Quaker meetings and at home they pray for Jim, and their loss seems greater as there is no body to bury, and no grave to mourn over. No parents should have to mourn their dead child. Yet many did.

Meanwhile, the military recruiters targeted the poor youth of the country, the so called poverty draft.

The Poverty Draft

Taken from street corners
Playing kick can with their mates
Taken from their mothers arms
To fight the evil
The evil man creates

Whisked away to foreign lands
With n'ere a chance to grow
Taken to that place
Where no school bell
Could save them
From their foe

No giggles now
Nor sharing cigs

Behind the bicycle shed
But hearing sorrow
Heavily falling in trenches
With the dead

What then the boy
Who cries for home
What now the boy
Who dies alone

So Arthur lost his brother in the very situation he had been
dreading. The futile loss of young life had happened to him,
despite all his campaigning, protesting and struggling to make
his opinions felt. Arthur did not give in and despite aggressive
opposition, he kept his faith in order to expose the evils of the
universal war machine.

Fascism
Comes creeping
in the night
while we sleep
and the planet
now lies weeping
for those
souls
we could not keep

II: 15 CASHMERE ROAD, EDGELEY, STOCKPORT

A few streets away in another part of Edgeley, Stockport, in another semi-detached house live Emily and Miles Smith. They come from a middle class background and are Methodists. Miles is a clever engineer and won a scholarship to attend Manchester University to study Engineering. They are very much in love.

Emily is very beautiful, with massive brown eyes and brown hair so long that she can sit on it. They are married and have one lovely daughter called Marjorie. Marjorie Smith was then Arthur Slater's girlfriend.

Below: Emily and Miles Smith

They had first met before the start of the war, at Gawsworth House in Abergele at a Quaker meeting, and had fallen in love. Marjorie who is my mother, also came from a peace loving family and said that in all the time that she lived at home with her parents, she never once heard them argue or shout at each other. The Smiths and Slaters were just two families who liked to live harmoniously with their neighbours, yet suddenly find themselves thrown into the depths of war.

Marjorie Aged 18 Years

Miles has a workshop in his cellar where he enjoys making and repairing clocks and watches and Emily loves playing the piano. Now the cellar must become their shelter from the bombings, rigged out with all the essentials for survival. Emily plays the piano whenever she can to keep the family spirits high.

So the family retreat to the cellar each night. After several peaceful nights with no imminent threat from the enemy, the family are lulled into a false sense of security and decide to risk sleeping in their beds. However that night the enemy unleashes incendiary bombs on Edgeley. Incendiary bombs weighing just a couple of pounds were the most destructive of all the bombs.

These bombs were just 18" long and were dropped by the basket load. They were dropped in clusters to spread fires. When they made contact with their target they spun around spraying out highly combustible chemicals such as magnesium phosphorus or petroleum jelly, otherwise known as napalm. An average of 72 of these bombs were dropped at one time.

Marjorie is awoken in the middle of the night by a tremendous crash and sits up in bed. She screams as an incendiary bomb lands at her feet at the bottom of her bed. The bomb starts to whirl around and sends a spray of its deadly contents into the room. Her mother and father rush to her room to find out the cause of the screaming. Emily grabs Marjorie, who is frozen in fear and Miles rushes to the bathroom, where the night before they have filled the bath full of water in case of such an emergency.

With buckets and bowls they form a small human chain and

manage to douse the flames which have now taken hold, and miraculously extinguish the bomb. Many people died when these bombs were dropped as the fire service was already overstretched and there was just no way to quell the fires. The family is thankful that there were no fatalities, and retreat to the cellar to spend the rest of the night. For the duration of the war they never again risk sleeping upstairs in their bedrooms.

Arthur, still mourning his lost brother is summoned to court to explain why he will not fight. The law states that: 'A conscientious objector be conscientiously opposed to the planned and organized killing that takes place in warfare.' The judge underestimating his intelligence, asked Arthur what he would do if a German came into his house and threatened his family and friends.

Arthur had done his homework and knew that the willingness to use violence against another individual in order to protect yourself or your family and friends was not denial of a conscientious objectors claim. "Look mate" said Arthur to the judge in a fit of characteristic reckless bravado, "I'd rather stick a bayonet through you".

By this outburst Arthur was making his stand against the corruption of the Courts and the status quo. If he was going down it would not be without protest. Juries at this time were renowned for their prejudice and animosity towards the conscientious objectors philosophies and consequently were exposed as not giving fair trials. The judge sent him to prison for six months for contempt of court, after which he was sent to work in hospitals in Manchester. There he tended the sick and wounded, and bathed the brave pilots in salt baths. This was an attempt to relieve the pain of the horrendous injuries they had sustained, when their planes had caught fire. Then he was sent to Stockport to work in a hostel, delousing and bathing tramps. The authorities tried to demean and demoralize the conscientious objectors with this type of work. Some were sent to hospitals to act as guinea pigs. There they were actually injected with viruses, then monitored to see what effect the virus had on the recipient.

Syd Rushton was a good friend of Arthur's. They were both born in Stockport, Cheshire: Syd in Adswood in 1919 and Arthur in Edgeley, in 1920, and they grew up there. Syd was not a Quaker but was very sympathetic to their way of thought, and he too became a conscientious objector. His reason for being an objector was

"Because he did not believe in killing his fellow man."

Syd lived according to his beliefs and respected other peoples. Syd was a very caring and genuine man. Syd was strong in his credence, regardless of how people might judge him. The conscientious objectors had to be tenacious and steadfast, as they suffered many disparaging insults and attacks at the hands of the proletariat.

And so the insanity of the war continues. In their shelters, their dugouts, their cellars, the English people endure their hardships and sacrifices with steel wills and most amazingly, a strong sense of optimism, interspersed with black humour. It was this secret weapon that Hitler and the Germans could not understand, however astute their code breakers and spies were. When Hitler tried to break the morale of the English people he could not have known of their ability to laugh, even under extreme hardships and adverse conditions. The German propaganda campaign bombarded the English airwaves with arrogant messages. These were intended to fill the English with desperation, in an attempt to make them surrender. Lord 'Haw Haw' always started his broadcasts with 'Jairmany calling , Jairmany calling'. My family sat in their cellar and made fun of the broadcasts.

William Joyce alias 'Lord Haw Haw', was born in New York in 1906, and when only a young child moved to Ireland where he was educated in a convent. It was there, that in a fist fight his nose was broken, and because it did not set properly he consequently spoke with a nasal drawl. This earned him the name of 'Lord Haw Haw.' Joyce was a member of one of the pre-war fascist groups in England where he stirred up anti-Semitic racism. In 1923 he joined The British Fascisti, Ltd and in 1932 joined Oswald Mosley's, British Union of Fascists.

They dressed menacingly all in black and were known as 'The Black Shirts'. They stood on street corners preaching their anti-semitic doctrines in order to incite conflict. Often vicious and terrible fights occurred at these rallies. The Battle of Cable Street is a sad but heart rendering example of the British fight against Fascism, in the David and Goliath scenario which took place there. On Sunday October 4th 1936, Mosley planned to march down Cable Street into the Jewish quarter of the East-End of London, to speak and agitate the Jewish community. However, before he could reach his destination, the good people there rallied together to block off the road with upturned lorries, mattresses and furniture. The Jews, the Irish and the British stood shoulder to shoulder to block Mosley's route. Children threw marbles in the path of the oncoming horses, which felled them and women threw missiles of milk bottles and whatever they could find from the above tenement flats and houses.

They chanted "ils ne passeront pas" (they shall not pass), the same chant used by the 'mob' in the French Revolution. Although there were many fist fights, injuries from police battons and object missiles 'The Black hand gang' did not get through and Mosley and his men had to retreat. This was certainly a victory for Democracy in Britain.

The steel will and determination of the good British people had won through. Their reaction to injustice was to be outraged and to fight for those who were mistreated with hearts of oak.

In 1939 Joyce fled to Germany where he immediately joined Joseph Goebbels Propaganda ministry and became a broadcaster. His radio programme reached England weekly from 1939 to 1945. On April 30th 1945, in Berlin, Joyce was arrested whilst giving a last drunken speech. He was returned to England where he was tried for treason.

Despite his plea for absolution on the grounds that he was an American citizen, Joyce was condemned on the grounds that he held a British passport. He was found guilty of treason and was hanged on January 3rd 1946.

III: TEARS OF SALT WATER

Meanwhile the conscientious objectors continue their campaigning for peace. *A Peace Pledge Union was set up and this stated that 'the conscientious objector has no right to reject war in the present unless he spends his life time in helping to make a future without war.'

Marjorie and Arthur, and Arthur's mother and father Edith and Hampson, hold Pacifist meetings and the Society of Friends set up the Friends Relief Service to help the victims of war. This service provided social welfare for families and people in need. The Friends Relief Service sent their members to wherever they were needed, to families who had suffered the devastation of losing their loved ones and their homes. They provided clothes, food, shelter and moral support for these people.

* 1934 The Peace Pledge: "War is a crime against humanity. I renounce war, and am therefore determined not to support any kind of war. I am also determined to work for the removal of all causes of war"

Most of the conscientious objectors were employed in humanitarian services, working for the fire brigade, on the ambulance teams, in the hospitals and in social care. In their own way they tried to perpetuate the British way of life and the sense of justice that they believed in.

When criticized and attacked for their beliefs Marjorie and Arthur find comfort and support in the writings and poems of the great pacifists, thinkers and philosophers of the world.

There is wisdom and truth yet to be found in a world of sorrow and pain. Despite the pressure of such adverse conditions, the love between Marjorie and Arthur grows stronger and they decide to marry. On the 6th March, 1943, they are married at Stockport Register Office. Arthur's profession is registered as a 'Tree Feller, (Timber Merchants) and Painter and Decorator', under the umbrella of 'Journeyman'. He is listed as a bachelor, of 23 years old, residing at 191, Old Chapel Street. Arthur was born on 26th April, 1920. Arthur's father is registered as Hampson Slater, a Railway Passenger Guard. Marjorie is registered as a spinster of 20 years old, and her occupation as that of 'Clerk' in the Co-operative Dairy in Stockport. Her home is registered as 15 Cashmere Road, Stockport, her father as Miles Smith and his profession as that of General Engineer. Marjorie was born on 7th September, 1922. Witnesses at the marriage were Marjorie's father, Miles Smith and Arthur's best friend and fellow conscientious objector, Syd Rushton.

On June 6th 1944, years of dedicated intensive organization culminated in Operation Overlord. D-Day had to be postponed several times as the weather conditions had to be absolutely perfect. There had to be a full moon to provide sufficient light, and a tide low enough to spot German placed obstacles on the shore and yet high enough for troops to avoid too much unprotected beach.

On the evening of 5th June 1944, the weather met all the required criteria and Eisenhower gave the signal "OK, Let's Go". For many of these men this was their final goodbye. Never again would they return to their homes. The majority of the men did not know what to expect and some attended mass on the crossing, some men were seasick and others managed to sleep, even though the conditions were cramped and uncomfortable. They were lambs to the slaughter and yet because of their bravery Hitler was defeated. The officers bustled about preparing maps and arranging landing stations. Some men sat under the stars, smoking, smoking, and wondering what was to become of them, whilst listening to the eerie silence that seemed to wrap itself around the brave boats, broken only by the intermittent creaking of the old hulls or the clanking of pipes from the boiler room.

The landing Craft Infantry towed barrage balloons for protection against German aircraft, but mercifully they were not needed. The convoy must have seemed surreal as it stealthily stole across the English Channel like a mother fox, aware of the great challenge ahead but driven on by the need to protect and feed its young.

I wonder if the ghost of Nelson
Was with them on that night
I would like to think
That he was there
To help them
In their plight

37

Slowly the dark night faded
Melted away from the ships
And the men
And for many
Of those dear brave souls
They would never
See home
again

Thin lines of pink and yellow light appeared along the horizon and Normandy was in sight. There was only one way to go now, and forward went those brave men. American, Canadian, and British men joined together in a bitter and terrible struggle to overpower the German forces.

The fighting was fierce and the allies suffered great losses, more than 10,000 men were killed in the battle, 6,603 of them were American.

Place of No Sorrow

And the sea held those precious bodies
Those fathers, those lovers, those sons
Their eyes holding tears of salt water
While they danced to the tune of the guns
They tumbled and rolled with the pebbles
Those brothers those uncles those braves
Some wearily crashing onto the beach
Some clamped in watery graves
Return to your homelands and loved ones
Please don't die on this Godforsaken beach
Return to that place of no sorrow
Where your sweetheart's arms
Are within reach

One remarkable story of bravery and courage is that of the Scottish Bagpiper, William Millin.

William Millin was born in Glasgow on the 14th July, 1922. On June 6th 1944 he was just 21. William was serving with the 1st Commando Brigade, when he was ordered by his commanding officer, Lord Lovat, to play the bagpipes on their arrival at Sword Beach in Normandy. The English army had banned the playing of the bagpipes during battle. Lord Lovat reasoned that because both he and William were Scottish it did not affect them.

As the German artillery pierced and perforated the English and American Troops, William Millin walked up and down the beach playing his bagpipes. Among the songs he played on that June day were 'Blue Bonnets over the Border', 'Highland Laddie' and 'The Road to the Isles.' He witnessed his comrades falling all around him but still kept on playing. Eventually he realised that he was alone and he had to run to catch the troops up. He then piped the troops over Pegasus Bridge on to the main land. Later on Millin talked to a captured German officer who said they did not shoot him because they thought he was crazy.

I can only think of what an inspiration William must have been to his comrades, how he must have kept their spirits strong, and how on that day he himself formed a bridge to the spirit world for his comrades to pass over. He died on August 17th, 2010. The French awarded him the 'Croix d'Honneur'. This is a French order established by Napoleon Bonaparte on 19th May 1802. The order's motto is Honeur et Patrie "Honour and Fatherland". I hope William is still playing his bagpipes in heaven, just like the 'Piper at the Gates of Dawn'.

IV: THE 'CHINDITS'

Many of the men who had gone to fight for their country were suffering in unbelievable situations which were horrific, and can only be described as hell on earth. The psychological strain and subsequent terrors were almost too much to bear for some of the soldiers, and many of those who actually returned home suffered alone.

Of all the accounts of the endurance and bravery of these soldiers few are as harrowing as those of the men who were sent behind Japanese enemy lines in Burma. These men were known as 'Chindits'. It was an expedition organized by Brigadier Orde Charles Wingate and the soldiers were known as Wingate's Chindits. This name was taken from the 'Chinthe' statues which were the silent sentinels to guard Burmese pagodas. The purpose of these statues was to ward off evil spirits that may be lurking in the jungle.

The first expedition went to fight the Japanese in Burma and the war in the Far East, in February 1943. This was the first expedition of the 'Chindits.' It was very basic with only 3000 men, and a small number of mules, bullocks and elephants. .

The second expedition was on a much grander scale. A local lad from Madron travelled to Burma and fought in this campaign. His name was Edward John Strick, and he was born at 2 Hillside Row, in the small village of Madron in Cornwall. He was educated at Madron School and then at Heamoor School from the age of 11 years, until he left school at the age of 15 years. In 1939, at the age of twenty he joined the Battalion of the Duke of Cornwall's Light Infantry, as a Private Soldier and eventually volunteered to fight in Burma, where he joined the Chindits.

Edward Strick was seconded to No. 1 Squadron 45 Regiment Reconnaissance Corps of India Command, which was part of the 16th Infantry Brigade. Edward was in the 2nd expedition of the Chindits, which was on a far larger scale than the first. This time there were more than 20,000 British and commonwealth soldiers. Edward joined 'Operation Thursday' in March 1944 and set off with these other brave men. He was then known as Trooper Strick. His Commanding Officer was Brigadier Bernard Fergusson (an ex Black Watch Officer). The Chindits were taken in to Burma, by Dakota's or glider aircraft, and dropped behind enemy lines. Burma was overrun by the Japanese and this was the second largest airborne invasion of the war.

Edward's job was to man a heavy machine gun which was transported by mule pack. The men also had to each carry a load of at least 72lbs or 33 kg of provisions. They had to hike up and down the jungle terrain in temperatures of often 40 degrees Celsius. In the monsoon season they had to cope with the treacherous mud underfoot, with mules and animals and themselves sliding all over.

Eddy looked after the mule. He even slept next to it in case it woke in the night. In that event he would have to feed it to stop it braying. In some other columns mules were not so lucky and had their vocal chords cut to keep them quiet. Eddy cared for the mule really well and suffered much anxiety when eventually they were forced to eat it or face starvation. The troops were constantly living on their nerve ends, and in one particular skirmish with the Japanese, Eddy was saved from death by his mess-can in his backpack which deflected a bullet. Thankfully for Eddy the Japanese were renowned for randomly firing into the air.

The Chindits were well trained and ready for war and hardships, but I doubt that they were really aware of the full extent of the horrors which lay ahead for them.

The troops had no proper rations. Theoretically the rations were to be dropped from the supply planes regularly. However dropping bundles of food into a vast jungle, often under gunfire whilst trying to hit an allocated destination was extremely difficult. Often the food drops were taken by the Japanese or the Burmese villagers. Of the men who did manage to return to Blighty most were just skin and bone, just mere skeletons.

The men had to manoeuvre their way through the jungle, often having to cut, slash, and tear their way through the vegetation. One of the hardest plants to tackle was known as elephant grass which grew by the water to an average height of fifteen foot high, was sharp as razor blades and spanned for miles. Yet this obstacle had to be overcome, as often the men could see the smoke of Japanese camps nearby, and there was no other safe route. Many of the maps that the men had been given were misleading and vague, and some were actually inaccurate. Often they would reach the top of a hill, only to find that in front of them lay undulating hills of jungle where the laborious process would have to start all over again.

They were under constant threat of being ambushed by the Japanese, who would suddenly appear from the bushes brandishing bayonets, with blood curdling screams which shot terror into the hearts of the men. They were outnumbered 10 to 1 by the Japanese. In addition to this horror, they also had to deal with wild beasts, tigers, snakes, tropical diseases, thirst, hunger and flies on their wounds.

One of the harshest dictates and one which considerably lowered the morale of the troops was that of having to leave their wounded comrades behind. The wounded were left on their own to die, left to the mercy of the Japanese and the jungle. Often when found by the Japanese these men were used as live bayonet practice.

One of these men who was wounded and left by his column was Ian MacHorton. He was nineteen when he joined the Chindits in Burma. In an horrific ambush he was wounded in the leg, and could not walk. Ian was carried by two of his friends and left beside a tree in a clearing overlooking the road to Mong Mit. In his pocket he found a printed text that his mother had sent to him in the last letter that he had received from her. In her letter she had written that there might be times when "he might need some extra help".

It was a quotation from M. Louise Haskins, 'The Gate of the Year'

* "I said to the man who stood at the gate of the year: 'Give me a light, that I may tread safely into the unknown' And he replied: 'Go out into the darkness and put your hand into the hand of God. That shall be to you better than a light and safer than a known way!' "

And with this new-found courage and faith, Ian did walk out of that jungle. He survived to write an amazing book about his story. The book is called 'Safer Than a Known Way'. This book is an account of Ian's ordeal, and his experience of being left on his own in the Burmese jungle. He suffered the fate of many other soldiers. They were taken to these places to fight and in the end many were deserted: left on their own to make their own way back home, if they could.

Trooper Strick was left to make his way back home on his own as well. When he did eventually return, a message in the small village of Madron was relayed back to his mum: "Your son Eddy is down at the village shop". Eddy had the same mental strength and determination that Ian also possessed, that true grit, inherent in their psyche which told them they were not going to be defeated.

Eddy's mother had heard no reports, from or of him, since she had received a poignant handmade card for the Christmas of 1944, dated 6/11/44, and so had presumed he was dead.

* Extract from 'The Gate of the Year' by Minnie Louise Haskins. Copyright © Minnie Louise Haskins, 1908. Reproduced by permission of Sheil Land Associates Ltd.

Eddy's handmade Christmas card sent: 6/11/1944

That is why, on his return to Madron, Eddy had waited at the village shop, thinking the shock would have been too much for her. Eventually, friends made their way down to the village shop to escort Eddy back home to his mother.

Planets spin
In the universe
Oscillating on pendulums
Of time
Whilst humans
Kill other humans
Their egos
Justifying
The crime

So we hear the stories from the men who return home, wounded and dying in this one arena on this planet of war. We do not hear the stories of those who do not return. Theirs are lost forever in the dark jungles and chronicles of time.

In 'War and Peace' written by Leo Tolstoy of the period 1805 to 1820, Tolstoy reflects on war. One of his characters 'Princess Marie' says of the troops leaving for the Napoleonic War.

"You should have seen the state of the mothers, wives and children of the men who were going, and heard them sobbing. It seems as though humanity has forgotten the precepts of its divine Saviour, Who preached love and forgiveness of injuries, and that men ascribe the greatest merit to the art of killing one another".

Despite the horrendous slaughter on the Normandy beaches, the surviving allies struggled on to fight against the Germans, and on 25th August 1944 Paris was liberated. As the war drew to a close many of the conscientious objectors continued the work they had begun, and went to work in the war torn cities of Europe. The Quaker Friends Relief Service went to where ever they were needed.

News was reaching England of the holocaust, the grotesque black evil that had enveloped parts of the world, and had manifested itself in its captives minds, their thoughts and eventually their actions. Six million Jews were murdered by the Nazis. On 27th January 1945 Auschwitz concentration camp was liberated, and now this day will always be remembered as 'Holocaust Memorial Day'.

A stone has been erected in Hyde Park Memorial Garden in London. The inscription on the stone reads, in both English and Hebrew: "For these I weep. Streams of tears flow from my eyes because of the destruction of my people". This is a quotation from the Book of Lamentations, Chapter 1: verse 16. The stone was described, by the then Environment Secretary Patrick Jenkin, as "a reminder of the past and a warning for the future".

On 30th April, 1945, the very same day that Lord Haw Haw was arrested, Hitler killed himself in Berlin. On May 7th 1945, the Germans surrender.

However Japan still posed a threat to America and Britain and on August 6th and 9th 1945, atom bombs were dropped on Hiroshima and Nagosaki.

Did insanity

Reach out and touch

Our inner

Mental sphere

Did the world

Stop turning

As we fell

Into the atmosphere

Did the sky

Slide back

And the face

Of God appear

Hiroshima Nagosaki

There is no explanation

Can there ever

Really be

Justification

In war truly, there are no winners. Everyone loses. In the madness of the human race great and beautiful cities of the world along with their inhabitants are burnt, plundered, destroyed, annihilated and reduced to cinders. Such was the fate of London, Berlin, Coventry, Nuremberg, Manchester, Dresden, Plymouth and so on and so on and so on.

The troops returned home to find that life was hard for them. After the initial Victory celebrations, they found that the dead were honoured yet those who had fought and survived, and even those who were badly wounded, were forgotten.

They were tormented with visions and memories of the horrors of war, and they no longer hated the conscientious objectors but actually acknowledged their inverted bravery. Many of them felt abandoned and alone and many suffered psychological traumas.

So Marjorie and her mother and father, Emily and Miles and Arthur and his mother and father Edith and Hampson had survived the war. They all mourn the loss of Jim, and Arthur realizes that he is lucky to be alive as during the First World War, conscientious objectors were condemned to death. The faith of the Methodists and Quakers had kept both sides of the family strong during the war.

V: THE WOODCUTTERS

The Healing Has Begun

The Seasons tumble past
Green turns to brown
To rust
To grey
Lives tumble past
In peaceful disarray

And they begin
To mend those lives
To put together
The broken pieces
To heal the wounds
That war inflicts
As now the fighting ceases

And somewhere
In a sun kissed clearing
On leaves and heather
And moss
An angel
Lies weeping
For
Brave souls
That were lost

The war now behind, Britain could move forward. The wounds of the mother fox were horrendous, and she stumbled and sought rest to lick and heal her wounds. Hitler had destroyed a part of British life, a part of our heritage had gone forever and would never return. Society became hedonistic and religious values, ethics and morals were all challenged.

Marjorie and Arthur on honeymoon in
Colwyn Bay North Wales

Now Marjorie and Arthur celebrate the end of the war with a belated honeymoon in Colwyn Bay, North Wales. Arthur obtained a job there in North Wales, working for the Forestry commission at Dolgellau.

Arthur also had the job of guarding Italian prisoners of War. At Dolgellau they rented a cottage from a farmer called Einion who lived nearby and they called the cottage Cae-Einion.

Cae-Einion Cottage North Wales - Cader Idris in the background, Circa 1945

Syd Rushton, Arthur's good friend and fellow conscientious objector joined Marjorie and Arthur to live at Cae-Einion. They also met other men who shared their ideals and philosophies and two of these men, Ray Perry and Reg Hemmes became friends, and joined them in the cottage. The men all worked together, planting and felling trees for the Commission. They formed a working party who daily went out into the forest and were known as the 'Woodcutters'

Cader Idris Mountain: View from Cae-Einion cottage

These men stayed with Marjorie and Arthur at Cae-Einion, and when they returned from work Marjorie would have lit the fire and the smell of freshly baked loaves would permeate the cottage. Later on Biddy Picard also joined them in the cottage.

Biddy Picard was born in Derbyshire and went to Art College in Chesterfield. She then went on to study at the Slade during the war, where she met the son of Augustus John, Casper John who was also studying there. Biddy then obtained a post of teaching at Badminton College in Bristol. Whilst she was on holiday from teaching she visited her parents who were staying in Lynmouth. There in a chance encounter she met the 'Woodcutters'. When she returned to her flat in Bristol she was delighted to receive a large box of daffodils from them.

The next time Biddy saw the 'Woodcutters', they did not see her. Biddy had travelled to North Wales and there as she sat on top of the mountain, Cader-Idris, she saw them walking in the valley below.

The woodcutters loved to yodel. They would yodel on their way to work, throwing their voices around the hillsides. They liked to yodel by the side of the lake, because it echoed around the valley. Biddy heard them yodeling and they made a great impression on this beautiful young girl.

Yet this time she did not say hello, she did not let them see her and let them pass by to their cottage. The party was made up of Arthur Slater, Ray Perry, Reg Hemmes and Syd Rushton. The woodcutters were stunning in their appearance. They were all handsome men, their bodies were bronzed with all the fresh air and sunshine and their muscles toned from all the axe wielding and climbing trees. Their spirit was unique and infallible, they embraced the whole world with the joy of life and freedom. Each day there was peace. Their voices no longer hit the walls of the dug outs, the shelters or the cellars but soared to the sky and back.

Carbon To Carbon

I hear their yodeling, here they come
Their axes glistening in the cold sun
Back to bond with the trees and the crows
To find their roots I suppose
And if you cut me down today
Will I cry or try
To run away

If a howling wind should blow me down
Then to the elements
I must yield
My body lying slain
Sixty foot
Across the farmers' field
My being ripped
Reluctantly
From the sodden ground
my roots exposed
redundantly
cruelly
placenta round

So chop me up to
burn on your fires
At least I can leaves drop
On your dreams and desires
I can whirl and spark
Like a manic banshee
And crackle and spit
Whilst making your tea
And then I will forgive you
Whilst I listen
to your woody jargon
For beneath our very souls
Are we not all
Just carbon to carbon?

Biddy eventually joined Marjorie and the group in Cae-Einion. These two beautiful young women, with their long flowing hair, gypsy skirts and often bare feet, certainly made an impact on the locals. These women made all their own clothes from any material they could find, even from curtains. Biddy can remember a particular favourite skirt made from a black cotton interspersed with red roses. They would braid flowers and leaves into their hair and clothes and often the locals would ask them if they were in a circus. The men wore army surplus clothes, cast off leather jackets with the sleeves cut out for working and khaki trousers.

The group all had enquiring minds, they were intellectuals and they were eager to learn. A man called Alf Knowles had the cottage originally and he inspired them to read esoteric books. Ray had been to university to study. Syd and Arthur came from working class backgrounds in Stockport, Cheshire, and they both had an inherent philosophical desire for knowledge. Arthur had also attended Art College in Stockport.

Their philosophies had helped to get them through. In the small cottage at Ca–Einion, the inhabitants discussed art, politics, religion, society and the state of mankind in the aftermath of the war. Their new environment was a catalyst and springboard for their artistic characters, and their search for knowledge and learning.

The days were spent creatively. The men worked outdoors chopping wood and the women worked equally as hard at their jobs inside the cottage, cooking and cleaning. They all read avidly, and lived frugally on a healthy diet of eggs, cheese, salad and homemade bread.

The veil of war that had hung over their lives had been lifted and new horizons began to appear through the mists. The bars of the prison of war had been broken. They had escaped from their cellars, they were alive, they were free.

The existence of the group was very basic and when they first moved into the cottage of Cae-Einion, they had no furniture. From Stockport they did take with them the possessions which they did cherish, their books, most prized. They slept in sleeping bags on top of piles of bracken and pine needles on the floor. When the bracken and pine needles needed changing, they swept it out and replaced it with new. They had a large wood burning stove which they fed with gorse and literally anything that would burn. The stove was iron and had a baking oven in the wall, which was ideal for the bread making. There was also a small fire upstairs in one of the bedrooms. The winter that the group moved in was bitterly cold. There was constant snow in North Wales. In the roof, above the stairs was a small hole. One morning Biddy walked out of the bedroom to find that the whole stairs was covered in a carpet of snow. The wind had blown the snow through the tiny hole.

There was no running water in the cottage but there was a stone sink in the lean-to at the back of the kitchen. There was a stream outside the cottage and their water was collected from there. That cold winter the stream was often covered in ice and they had to knock off massive chunks of ice before they could collect the water. When the fire was lit the kitchen was warm and cosy and often they would bring lambs in to keep them warm and to prevent the ravens from pecking the lambs' eyes out.

To collect the daily milk they had to trudge for one and a half miles. That cold winter was very beautiful in the mountains as the weather was icy and cold but sunny and dry, and my mother, Marjorie, said she could remember running naked through the snow to swim in a damn near the cottage. They were all very fit. They would walk and hike everywhere. Some evenings they would all walk from Cae-Einion to the cinema in Dolgellau. On their return, in the dark they would all link arms and sing. One false move and they would have plunged down the steep, rugged mountainside.

Biddy and Marjorie were happy to tend to the domestic chores in the cottage while the men went off to work on the Forestry Commission. However, when the woodcutters returned to their cottage every evening they threw their work clothes on the floor, for the girls to pick up and wash. The girls had enough work to do without this extra burden and threatened the lads saying "if you do this again we will burn them". Imagine the lads shock when they arose one morning to find that, true to their word, the girls had indeed burnt their work clothes.

The tough lifestyle at the cottage had made the girls resolute and strong in their spirits and characters. Every day they awoke to see through their windows the majestic mountain of Cader-Idris and the beautiful meandering fields and countryside, and so in their wildness and determination the group could celebrate their freedom.

VI: DESTINY

In the hollow of a silence
after the crashing of the trees
Destiny comes calling
from her home amid the seas
In her white dress she comes calling
from her hands the foxgloves falling
while all around the granite
whispers in the breeze
If you hide
she will find you
with her velvet gown
she will bind you
put your shattered past
behind you
and bow to Destiny
With the stars and moon
to guide you
and Destiny beside you
your strength will
always find you
sweet sister
Destiny

And in Cornwall, a stirring was beginning. It was a gathering of like-minded people all with social consciences and artistic leanings. They had all been through the war and survived, they were alive. They were free.

Warm sunbeams came down from heaven and stopped to rest momentarily on the wise Cornish granite, to bring healing and peace. Dreams of peace had become a reality and enveloped the souls that dwelt in the bodies that moved on the Cornish land. There was a feeling of being reborn, a feeling of peace on earth. The survivors were fortified by their struggle. They were rewarded with days of gentle softness. The dark days spent sheltering underground were gone and the world was becoming conscious of the possibilities of a new clearer space and time. Men vowed that never again should the planet experience such hatred and evil. Those who survived the bombings, the fascism, the pain and the futility of war, and the needless killing of the innocent, took stock of their lives and the meaning of life.

The legacy of the artists, the bohemians, the woodcutters, writers and painters who migrated to Cornwall after the Second World War, to live in truth and peace, is still unfolding. The artists way of life was calling to them: working and painting outside in the fresh air, sleeping under the stars. This bohemian romantic lifestyle was a world away from the worries and torments of war. It was an escape to a new life and a new beginning. They were all very spiritual beings and possessions did not mean a great deal. They shared what they had and did not want material gain. There was a tremendous feeling of comradeship. People roamed the countryside and stayed anywhere. They would sleep in barns, in railway stations, safe in the knowledge that the enemy had been beaten. People would open their doors to each other and embrace each other as if to say with faith we made it through.

News of a particular idyllic artist colony in Lamorna, Cornwall reached the occupants of the cottage at Cae-Einion in Wales. Biddy decided to leave Wales and in 1945 she actually walked down the Welsh coast from Dolgellau to Milford Haven with Syd Rushton. At one point Biddy recollected that she felt so tired that she decided to rest in a railway station waiting room. There was a big open fire in the waiting room and it was packed with families just keeping warm. These people had lost their homes in the bombings and many families were nomadic, wandering around the land looking for a place to set up a new home. On that particular night there were no seats left so Biddy put her sleeping bag on the table and slept there. The railway guards came in, banked up the fire and allowed them to sleep there the whole of the night.

Eventually Biddy and Syd reached Milford Haven. In the harbour they were resting and leaning on some railings when some French fishermen came out of the Post Office. Biddy and Syd asked them where they were going and when they said to Newlyn, they asked if they could have a lift. So they hitched a lift on this Bretton Crabber with a crew of three French fishermen. It was a tiny boat with a Kelvin engine. The fishermen were literally starving. They were stewing a cormorant and as a substitute for coffee were drinking burnt wheat. They had few possessions, and when Biddy was tired and wanted to rest, all they could find for her to lay her head on was an old map. When they eventually arrived in Newlyn, the Harbour was full of French crabbing boats just like the ones painted by Van Gogh. They must have looked so pretty in the harbour all painted in their bright blue colours. The French fishermen went collecting snails from the cliffs and would put them in hankies, and boil them. They wore navy jerkins and it was them who first brought the fashion of the Fishermans' smock to Newlyn.For Biddy the move from the dark moody mountain of Cader Idris to the beautiful opalescent light of the Cornish landscape was welcoming and inspirational.

From there Biddy made her way to Lamorna. My mother and father stayed for two more years in Wales and in 1947, they also moved to Lamorna. So now the artists' colony also incorporated the Woodcutters. They lived on the cliffs there, and slept in sleeping bags under the heavens. When it rained they slept under Biddy's gypsy caravan, as she was already living there.

The men would carry very sharp axes for their work, with blades of 6 to 9 inches long. The men had long hair and beards and together with the women the locals can remember that they were a colourful band. The locals called them 'Billy Goats' because of their beards and can remember them swimming in the nude off Carn Duan. Vernon Roberts is a local man, who still lives in Madron. He was fourteen when the 'Woodcutters' came to Cornwall, and he can remember the impact that they had on the area, and especially on the women. It was similar to the effect that the American troops had on them.

Although the 'Woodcutters' did not call the women 'honey', or buy them silk stockings, they still impressed them with their wild bohemian attitude towards life and their full beards. Vernon says that previous to the arrival of the 'Woodcutters' in Cornwall, the majority of Cornishmen were clean shaven. They worked hard all week in the fields, down the mines and on the sea. On Sundays they would be spruced up and clean shaven to attend Chapel. The influence of the 'Woodcutters' meant that they now had poetic license to grow beards.

Later on Vernon also had the courage to grow his own beard. Since Methodism had swept Cornwall with the influence of John and Charles Wesley, beards had been regarded as a symbol of Paganism. Now communities became more relaxed in their attitudes, realising that this appearance did not necessarily mean a return to the bad old days of heathenism and witchcraft.

Bill Picard had been serving in Burma for ten years up until the end of the war. He returned to England, and sitting in a warm reading room of a library in London, he read of a colony of artists in Cornwall, at a place called Lamorna. Bill decided that that was where he would go.

Bill had been told by a gypsy that his destiny was with a woman he would meet on a beach. This lady would symbolise Aphrodite coming out of the water. This gypsy even drew a picture of a lady coming out of the sea.

When Bill arrived at Lamorna he went down to the cove. There he saw Biddy coming out of the sea. He had met his Aphrodite. Bill and Biddy fell in love and lived on the cliffs in a gypsy caravan and cooked on camp fires.

Syd Rushton also met his Aphrodite in Lamorna: a lady called Jean, and together they lived on the cliffs, in a second camp between Lamorna and Carn Bargus. Syd and Jean actually met in Lamorna Cove. Syd managed to obtain a gypsy caravan and they lived in that. Although the outside of the caravan did not have flowers or images it was painted

65

brightly in green, yellow and red. The caravan furniture was fitted and was decorated with painted vine leaves. There were little painted drawers, and a bed with an upstairs part for the parents and an underneath part for the children with sliding doors which could be closed during the daytime. The effect was very fitted and very tidy.

Syd and Jean would walk to the nearest water supply, and depending on where they were, this could have been a river, stream or tap. It might have been close or a little distant. Jean can remember carrying a lot of buckets of water when the children were young. Jean did not make all her own clothes but sometimes would make or adapt something when she discovered nice pieces of fabric. She also did this for the children and can remember making waistcoats for the children. Jean is very artistic and loves beautiful things.

On a hot day in July, serenaded by the sea, the sun, the wildflowers, a sense of freedom and hope for the future, Syd and Jean's son was born outside the caravan. It was a natural birth with the aid of a midwife and they called their son Heath. In good weather Jean cooked outside on an open fire but when the weather turned bad they cooked inside the caravan on the small black coal burning stove. The caravan also had fitted gas lamps. It must have been so romantic and cosy in the evenings watching the sun set over the sea and the Scilly isles. However it would have been a completely different world when the turbulent seas roared and the forceful winds blasted against the cliffs and the little caravan.

Marjorie and Arthur continued to sleep under Biddy's caravan. As the hedonistic hot days of summer, turned to cool autumn afternoons, then to cold winter nights with biting gales and drenching rain, they found it increasingly difficult to sleep there anymore. They dug a trench under the caravan and covered themselves with tarpaulin. One evening a terrible storm battered the cliffs at Lamorna and Marjorie and Arthur realized they could no longer live in this way. That night they managed to stay in a friend's shed at the bottom of their garden.

The caravan under which Marjorie and Arthur found refuge

Susan, John and Marjorie at the cottage steps

Dale Cottage

VII: BOSWARTHEN

As Marjorie and Arthur were now homeless. they decided that the best course of action to follow would be to return to their parents in Stockport. There, they would be able to cope safely with the arrival of their first born child.

So this is what they did and on September 19th 1947, Susan was born in Stockport. Later that year Arthur returned to Cornwall to search for a home for his family. He returned to Lamorna to work at carpentry, sculpting and painting.

It was there that one of his friends, Stan Gardner, told him of a cottage that he knew of on the Bolitho Estate that was available for rent. This was the only cottage at Boswarthen that was owned by the Bolitho Estate, the rest of the cottages in the hamlet were tithe.

Arthur went to Boswarthen to see the *cottage. The fact that it was without electricity or sanitation did not deter Arthur as he was desperate to provide a home for his family. Stan and Arthur took out the first floor of the cottage to make the place light and airy and ideal for Arthur to paint and sculpt. The cottage was believed to be over 4oo years old and the rent then was six shillings and eight pennies a week. The cottage had a panoramic view of the surrounding countryside, Mounts Bay and St. Michaels Mount. It was a few fields away from the old Celtic Baptistery and Wishing Well, and to the North East, the ancient monument of Ding Dong mine. Arthur's fair maiden and child were then brought to their new home. Marjorie and Arthur still held the vision of the romantic bohemian arty lifestyle but the reality was far from this. Officials were sent to inspect the cottage and it was condemned as unfit for human habitation. However Arthurs' father Hampson, came to visit from Stockport. He and Arthur built a shelter at the bottom of the garden and installed an Elsan toilet in it, and my family were allowed to stay.

The Elsan toilet was simply a large metal drum with a toilet seat on top. When it was full, a hole had to be dug in the adjoining field and the contents emptied. When Sue was learning to talk, she couldn't say Arthur and she couldn't say lavatory, so she called the toilet 'Arses Latatry', as she had seen Arthur and grandfather building it. There was no running water in the cottage and drinking water had to be collected from the well which was situated up and along the lane at the top of the farm, behind Boswarthen Farm house.

---

*A Local historian believed that Dale cottage was one of the oldest dwellings in West Penwith. In the 15th Century under an ancient law 'He who built a house between sunset and sunrise, with walls, roof and smoking chimney, could claim the freehold. He could also claim the land as far as he could throw an axe. These houses were known as 'Ty unnos' This means house built overnight.'

www.snowdonia-society.org.uk

Marjorie collecting the water from the well: Note Boswarthen Farm House which lies opposite Dale cottage

Immediately outside the cottage were large granite steps which led up to a field. At the top of the steps, on the left hand side was a tank which caught rain water, but this could only be used for washing, The field outside the cottage rose gently to join other fields which eventually led to Madron Carn.

Susan, John and Marjorie in the field outside the cottage

As the first floor of the cottage had now been removed the place was similar in construction to a barn. There was one door in the place, the main door. On entering through this low door your eyes were immediately taken up to the rafters and the wooden beams running towards the apex of the roof. The roof was made of grey slate tiles. On the opposite wall to the door and to the left there was a set of wooden stairs. This led to a platform with a small balcony of three feet high, which was the only bedroom. Above the door in the roof was a skylight window which leaked when the South Westerly gales brought storms and torrential rain. To the right of the door and high up in the wall was a window with a view of the fields, of Madron and the bay beyond and St. Michaels Mount. There were four windows downstairs: one tiny window looked across to the farmhouse, and the two slightly larger windows were on either side of the door and faced South across the fields towards Madron Carn. Then there was the tiny window which looked down the lane. My mother would watch from this window to check that I wasn't disrupting the serene siesta of the unsuspecting snails.

On entering the cottage to the left of the front door, there was a raised platform which served as a sitting area, across which mother hung an army blanket in an attempt to keep us warm. There was one huge redbrick fireplace in this area, with a huge rotund chimney breast which protruded into the room and continued its massive protrusion into the platform bedroom upstairs. The chimney pot on the roof was covered in ivy, and ivy grew all around the cottage. There was a small garden which was flanked with huge granite stones which formed the wall between the garden and the lane.

Above: The end of the cottage showing the open small window where Marjorie would keep a look out on snail patrol

73

John and Marjorie in the field outside the cottage...notice the ivy covering the chimney and the roof

Left: Susan, John and Marjorie...Right: John and Arthur both pictures taken in the field outside the cottage

So this was the basic shell in which Marjorie and Arthur and their little girl Susan, set up home, and they were happy in their little cottage. Though they had few possessions the cessation of war brought a rich calmness to the land and its inhabitants, covering the cottage, the countryside, the mines, the carn, the yellow gorse and the creatures of the earth, in a cloak of golden gossamer.

The hamlet of Boswarthen is two miles from the village of Madron. The village of Madron , takes its name from the celt, St Madern who is reputed to have come from Brittany in the sixth century. He landed on the shores of Mounts Bay and followed the stream to its source and there he built a baptistery. He built this on the stream so the water could run through the building. Here he provided a place for Baptism, and the water became famous for its healing qualities. It is this Baptistery which lies near the Wishing Well. Now the Baptistery is roofless but it is still used by the chapel and the Church for services.

Lanyon Quoit lies to the North West and the ancient Ding Dong tin mine lies to the North East of Madron. The mine is now abandoned and the old mine workings are filled in. The mounds of the dump are still visible but they are now covered in grass, and grass grows up the side of the old engine houses, and the rough stone walling of the shaft heads. The sad, abandoned pumping station, with the tall chimney and the ghosts of the miners are all that remains. In the evening twilight the crows encircle the old chimney with their crazy cackling choruses and at night the rabbits run around the ruin.

The Phoenicians and the Greeks sailed to Mounts Bay to trade for metal and the name of one of the shafts at Ding Dong was Ishmael. The names of the other shafts were Jacobine, Killiow, Greenpeas and Tallow. Many travelers came from the Middle East in search of tin. Joseph of Arimathea was himself a tin trader, and some historians believe and many others would like to believe that he bought his nephew Jesus to Ding Dong mine. It is believed that Joseph of Arimathea was either Mary's or Joseph's uncle. It is possible that Jesus came with his uncle, not only to deal in tin but also to meet the Druids and exchange ancient knowledge and wisdom.

Just outside Madron is the carn. This was once a heavily wooded and rocky terrain, where Bronze Age man and then Iron Age man roamed, sheltered from the elements, and eventually settled. Evidence of their existence has been discovered in the form of burial tombs and barrows.

The granite remains of long lost villages that have lain sleeping for thousands of years, under beds of bracken and brambles, have been stumbled upon. These villages consist of circular dwelling houses made of a combination of granite walls and natural fibres for the roof. These houses were then circled around a large circular building which could possibly have been the Chieftains' house, or a central meeting house.

At one of these villages, fairly recently discovered near Lanyon Quoit, a lizard appeared at the entrance to a burial chamber, as if it were magically protecting the spirit of the deceased. Another of these surviving stones is Lanyon Quoit, which stands like a monstrous granite dragon, just a mile from the carn. This is one of the most famous of Cornish Antiquities. It is rumoured that before a great storm in 1815 when one of its granite legs was broken, it was about twelve foot high.

Marjorie and Arthur continued to be happy in their little home surrounded by all this beautiful heritage and countryside. On 26th of February of 1951 they have a son, whom they named John James Slater and who is actually born in the little granite cottage at Boswarthen. Then on Christmas Eve of 1952, I was also born in the little cottage in the Dale.

So Susan spent her formative years in this happy, creative environment, with her mother and father. She had both freedom and security. Arthur's parents paid for Susan to attend West Cornwall School, a private school in Penzance. The school held great kudos in International Educational levels, and many Heads of State in the Commonwealth sent their daughters to board at the school. From an early age Sue developed great confidence and from her father inherited artistic flair and vision. It was a blessing that Sue had this fortunate grounding in life. It made her strong and resilient Ten years later in that very same cottage in the Dale, she was going to need those characteristics, when our families' circumstance changed.

Arthur with Susan

VIII: DARK CLOUDS

Carn Kenidjack - 'The Hooting Carn'. A.C. Miles Smith

"The web of our life is of a mingled yarn, good and ill together"

All's Well That Ends Well (IV.III.83) - Shakespeare

Yet even under the blanket of peace the devil was lurking. He had loved the war, the hatred and the violence. The war had empowered him, it gave him authority and fuelled his dreams of world domination. He decided to camp at Carn Kenidjack also known as the hooting carn. During the day he disguised himself as one of the rocks, and at night while the moon electrified the land and giants scudded past pretending to be clouds he crept about the fields and the carn.

Darkness

The sky turned grey
The hounds did bark
And from the stone
Cast cold and dark
The devil himself
Did make his mark

He stirred himself
From his bed of stones
And stretched
And turned
His evil bones

Across the carn
He creaked and crept
Through bushes of gorse
And hawthorn
Windswept

He crept over to Ding Dong and the old mine. There he felt angry, he knew that Jesus had been to that very place when he was a boy, and that he had travelled there with Joseph of Arimathea. The creeping creature could sense the feeling of peace and love which pervaded the very grass and the hillocks and it annoyed him and made him feel sick. He knew that he could not stay there and that he must move on.

He continued his journey. He crept down from Ding Dong, down the track that led through the gorse bushes and the vetch. Down he stumbled, down the very same granite track that the cavemen had once trodden, dressed in furs and carrying their dead spoils of the hunt to roast on the fire.

The animals in the fields heard his hooves and smelt the blackness that preceded him. They hid in their burrows and lairs, huddled together, frightened to breathe. His hooves passed by and then they were safe.

He carried on down the bank until he came to a large farmhouse at Boswarthen. The dogs started to bark and he knew he dare not enter there.

Then he came across a small woodcutter's cottage. It was the size of a barn and the huge chimney was covered in ivy. He peeped in, through a tiny window. Inside he saw a beautiful lady asleep on a bed beside the fireplace. The dying embers of a log fire glowed faintly and in this low light he could see a Moses basket and sleeping peacefully in the basket, a baby. He chuckled to himself. He could do some mischief here. He disguised himself as a rock and hid in the moonlight, now and then dozing and now and then opening one fiery eye to check the surroundings.

In the morning the sun rose over St. Michaels mount and the birds began their daily songs. A pastel pink shiny aura covered the fields and the carn beyond as the universe spun its delicate thread of good and evil over the land.

Again he peeped through the tiny window and he watched as two small children came down from their beds on the shelf under the eaves. He saw the beautiful lady and the baby swaddled in love. He chuckled again and his tail swished in anticipation. Rich pickings here he thought.

He saw the love that the lady gave to her children and even though his heart was set in stone, he did feel for the first time ever, a twinge, so light, as if a spider had run over his heart. The sensation was momentary, like the blinking of his evil steel eyes and it passed forever.

He watched as a pickup truck drove up to the tiny cottage.

The children ran out in the crisp morning snow to greet the handsome man who stepped from the truck.

Arthur Slater was then in his prime. At five foot ten he was not that tall, but he was well built and rugged. He wore his golden brown hair long and combed back off his face. A few rogue strands of hair would nonchalantly escape and fall into his eyes. To women he seemed as some mythical creature in brown baggy corduroy trousers. He had a strong spirit and his very presence commanded respect.

He would not conform. The move to Cornwall and the influence of his artistic friends had made Arthur flamboyant and when in Penzance he would waltz down the terrace with his long hair flowing and a cravat tied around his neck.

The locals in Madron and Penzance nicknamed him 'Cap'n Arthur'. He was impetuous and boisterous. He once jumped into a horse trough to wash the mud off himself after a game of hockey. He was good at cricket as well and played for Madron. He would always knock the ball 'for six'.

The move to Cornwall had rejuvenated Arthur. The clear light inspired him. He was now painting, sculpting and creating wooden carvings and furniture. He rented a workshop in Penzance with a friend, where he carved the doors for the Admiral Benbow depicting Neptune, a dolphin and a mermaid. Consequently Arthur was spending more and more time in artistic circles and less and less time with his family.

Arthur did not stay long at the cottage that day. Fate was changing his path and the devil was watching from his hidden lair.

Arthur kissed Marjorie goodbye as she held the small bundle in her arms whilst the two small children held on to her skirts.

The children ran up to the bedroom window that looked down the fields into the bay. They saw their fathers' pickup truck getting smaller and smaller as its wound its' way down through the fields, and the along the lanes into the village of Madron and beyond into the town of Penzance.

No one saw the dark figure, crouched in the back of the pick-up truck, hidden under the logs.

The crisp cold winter day enfolded. Marjorie lit the log fire in the massive red brick fireplace and the family sat around. An icy wind started to blow across the land from the sea. As the last rays of the cardboard sun set behind the carn, the smoke from the cottage chimney puffed and billowed its signals into the cold air. The pale glassy sky gave forth the first diamond stars of the evening. The crows called and mocked and flew back to roost in the carn.

When Susan and John were tucked up in their little beds under the eaves, Marjorie sat by the fire with the baby. She wondered where Arthur was, it was getting late. The big brass oil lamp flickered on the old round table and the logs crackled on the fire.

Outside the soft snow had started to fall again, covering the granite stones in the garden and the path. The fields lay in long white rows of forgetfulness. The water in the tank froze.

On returning home later that night, to the shelter of his lonely rocks the evil creature approached the small cottage at Boswarthen. He peeped in through the small window. The curtains were drawn. A sudden blast of glacial wind rattled his old bones and blew across his back. He turned and crept away. His hoof prints were soon covered by the falling snow.

Nodding sleepily by the fire Marjorie heard the dogs at the farm barking, then silence descended again and she fell into a deep sleep.

Ebb & Flow

Across the land
We lived in
We dreamt
Our lives away
And seeing love
With all its power
We knew
We must obey

The laws of nature
Bind us
The coils of love
Entwine us
The sea of love
Surrounds us
Then ebbs
And flows away.

Yet at night
The fairies
And the pixies
Kept vigil
At the cottage door
Weaving their lanterns
To and fro
Across the fields
Up from the shore.

IX: 'AND THAT'S HOW WE LEARNED TO LIVE'

Marjorie and Arthurs' relationship now started to deteriorate. It seems that the sad irony of life often occurs when individuals strive and struggle to achieve a goal, but then having achieved that goal are forced apart by invisible and unforeseen circumstances. Often there are forces working in our lives, forces that are unseen, unknown, but very strong. These are often undercurrents that we are unaware of but which have great influence on us. They sweep and swirl us in the chaotic stream of life, then hurl us brutally onto the rocks.

Marjorie's days were now completely dedicated to caring for the children.

With no running water, no washing machine, only an open fire to dry clothes by, and only an Elsan toilet at the bottom of the garden, that in itself presented a mammoth task. She now had two small babies, a newborn infant and a toddler of one year and ten months, and Susan who was now five years old. Both babies would have been wearing nappies, the towelling ones that had to be washed by hand. If the weather was raining Marjorie could use the water from the tank for washing but then had to dry the nappies in front of the fire. If the weather was fine the nappies could be dried on the line but extra water had to be fetched from the well. The hardest task for Marjorie was collecting fire wood. If Arthur did not bring logs on his pick-up truck, Marjorie had to collect what firewood she could from the lanes and fields. This entailed pushing the baby in the pram, walking with Susan and brother John, (just a toddler at her side) and loading up the bottom of the pram with wood.

And that's how we learned to live. The old granite cottage was our shelter as the Cornish seasons were our tutors. Us babies grew fat and podgy on our mothers love, and the buttery sunshine. My mother was now without her husband and us children without a father, and just like the small flowers in the dark forest that struggle to grow, so we too struggled to grow towards the light. In the photograph of me as a toddler sitting on the old granite step of the cottage, I am wearing a pair of my brother's dungarees which are far too big for me and I looked worried. And that's how I remember growing up, always worrying about what was going to happen to us.

Occasionally Arthur would come to visit. Rumours would reach us that he had been seen in the town of Penzance or the village of Madron. Us children would sit for hours in the little granite window watching across the landscape for his arrival. The upstairs window was like a time travel machine, in that you could sit in the alcove of the window and draw the curtain behind you and dream.

When Arthur's truck was first spotted winding its merry way around the lanes and through the fields towards the cottage, great excitement would break out, and the children would run out into the garden to meet him. Arthur then had a pick-up truck and he had made a wooden canopy for the back. One day we saw the pick-up truck approaching but it seemed to disappear behind the hedge at the bottom of the lane nearest to the cottage. Eventually we went to investigate, to find the pick-up truck parked at the bottom of the little lane with both cab doors wide open.

There was Arthur, fast asleep across the two seats of the cab. His shirt was partially unbuttoned and underneath it something was moving. We peeped under his shirt to find the cutest, fluffiest wire haired fox-terrier puppy. Arthur had brought us children a present and we called her Judy. Judy enriched our lives. Where ever we children played, Judy was there. When the corn had grown taller than us children, in the field outside our cottage, we would play hide and seek with her. Mum would keep her in the cottage until we shouted 'ready', and then Judy would race around the field and always find us all.

Anna, Judy and John. Behind them the tree that Arthur planted when John was born. This tree is now taller than the cottage.

Another memorable day Arthur came to take us children to the beach, for a game of cricket. We all sat in the back of the pick-up truck and sang our heads off.

Arthur led the singing:

* "When the red red robin
Comes bob bob bobbin' along, along
there'll be no more sobbin'
when he starts throbbin' his old sweet song"

But then Arthur stopped visiting and I can remember sobbing. A great sense of emptiness and abandonment seemed to fall on me. Us children would still sit in the window looking out for his truck, but the visits now were very rare.

The last time Arthur came to visit, he had changed. He rode up the lanes in a red Austin convertible. He wore a brown sheepskin coat and was smoking a cigar. The cigar smoke pervaded the air of the tiny cottage bringing with it an unknown alien frightening atmosphere. The children sat on the old rickety bed that lay adjacent to the big red brick fire. The bed was covered in a patchwork blanket that their grandma had made. The children gazed into the fire, frightened to speak. Arthur sat directly in front of the fire on the small chair that mother called the nursing chair. It was a very low chair with a strong wooden back, and was ideal for breastfeeding babies. The deep blue velvet on the back of the chair was ripped and tattered and the stuffing from the padding was hanging out. Arthur did not notice this and he did not take his coat off. It was strange to have him sitting in our mother's chair. I felt embarrassed at our poverty and was subdued and quiet. I realize now that this was his final goodbye.

One morning, not long after this memorable visit Marjorie came up the ladder to our little shelf bedroom under the eaves to tell us that Arthur and her were to be divorced. She did her best to hide her sorrow and to keep the situation light. I was so upset and started to cry. I vowed to myself then, that I would never get married. There was no point in marriage I thought. Men just went off and left you. 'Happily ever after' had just been completely erased for me.

Then Arthur was gone with his swashbuckling flamboyance and my mother was left to cope on her own.

Yet our mother struggled on. We could dance with the butterflies and count the shining diamonds of the morning dew in the fields outside the cottage door. We could visit the farm across the lane and collect the milk which was a deep buttercup yellow and still warm from the cow, carrying it in a big white jug with a head of yellow cream.

We could play in the meadows and make a swing across the stream where the wild iris and watercress grew in abundance. We could dream in the sunshine on the banks where the fragrant primroses showed their pretty heads in Spring. In summer we could lie in the cornfield outside the cottage door, whilst watching the clouds scudding past feeling like we too were flying in the universe. And all this our mother wanted for us so that we had our freedom. She prayed that we never knew the horrors of years spent in dark cellars hiding from evil forces that had planned to take over the world.

The Mermaid

And in the darkness
she did sit
deep in deepest thought
and on that rock she pondered
where lay
the comfort
she sought

The planet
spun around her
beneath her
and above
the moon did light the night
and the sea did speak with love

go to your children
they need you so much now
hold them
wrap them in your heart
do not
let them go

and the waves did crash
and weave and wallow
then rush
and laugh and play
and twinkling moonbeams
caressed the water
as on the rock she lay

Into the velvet stream of water
she did slip and slide
and as the moon laughed down
on the sparkly planet
beneath the seaweed she did glide

and if
on magic moonlit nights
you sit beside the sea
and glimpse
a shimmering form
beneath the waves
you know who it will be

Dale Cottage showing the small bedroom window where I would sit and write my poems

* Arthur built a mezzanine bedroom area to the right hand side of the cottage door, thus allowing access to the window.

X: THE CREAKING CARN

And at night we could return to the cottage and the warmth of our mother's love. Then the big brass oil lamp would be lit on the old round wooden table, and we would sit around for our evening meal, which was cooked on the paraffin stove. Large black shadows loomed on the whitewashed walls behind us, as we ate our meal and the vast swirling seagull saturated universe contracted into our small reality.

When it was eventually time to go to bed, we would carry our little blue oil lamps up the ladder to our beds, to rest them beside the beds. Our beds were under the sloping eaves of the cottage on shelf like platforms that had waist high bannisters that you could look over and down into the cottage.* The bed shelf to the left of the cottage entrance door had stairs ascending to it, and one third of the way up these stairs, rested the ladder which then spanned across to permit access to the other bed shelf on the other side. At night we would lie in our beds under the sloping eaves. All that separated us from the Atlantic storms were some grey slate tiles and a layer of whitewash. We could hear the birds walking on the roof above, and ivy would often grow inside through the window frame. At night earwigs and woodlice would drop from the eaves onto the beds.

On cold winter nights the cottage was so cold that, in order to keep warm, we had to pile old coats on top of our beds. The only heating in the cottage was the open fire and as soon as that was extinguished the cold crept in. We had frost on the bedclothes.

On cold winter days often there was nothing to burn on the fire, and we children had to walk to the carn above the cottage to collect wood for the fire. Madron Carn lies above Boswarthen, just four fields away from Dale Cottage. The carn is a live magical place of serenity and peace, protecting the traveller with its thick arms of gnarled wood and thick dark leaves. In Spring the rhododendron trees would blossom and break forth their beautiful array of colour, so that when gazing southward from Boswarthen towards the carn, all the eye could see would be the sprawling canopy of light pastel pink and purple flowers.

In winter when the gales blew across the land the old rhododendron trees would sway, creak and crackle in the wind. Often there was snow, and the children must set off across the fields, the sweet notes of their chatter, bouncing and interweaving with those of the seagulls and the crows. The children dress in all the warm clothes they can find. The cold winter winds pierce the hedgerows in shivering blasts of stormy rage. The sea glistens and churns in the rays of the cold sarcastic sun, or lies defiantly harsh and untouchable, as if it were one gigantic frozen iced block of white wedding cake. The air is sharp on the rosy cheeks of the children. Now and then a soft flake of snow will settle on a little face. Glancing behind them to the cottage, the children can see the clothes hanging stiff and solid on the line.

And whisperingly

I wish to be

Lighter again than today

That I can float

And I am free

And I can fly away

Across the fields

Up to the carn

And beyond

To yesterday.

Now my memories of that cold air hitting the nostrils seem as sweet as champagne, but then as a child the air was cold and frightening as a dark rum. Yet once we reached the carn and we entered under the thick canopy of trees, we were protected by the foliage and the thick rhododendron leaves. The roaring wind was then outside, yet still trying to blow the creaking rhododendron trees down and invade our safe retreat. As we explored deeper into the thick undergrowth the wind became a wistful whisper. Beneath our feet lay a gentle blanket of sweet soft emerald moss, bordered in springtime by fragrant bluebells of lapis lazuli hue. Just for a while we children can laugh and play in our primitive shelter. Suddenly a fierce gust of wind can be heard above our inner sanctuary, and shivering we remember our duty and the struggle with the branches begins. My brother John must saw the biggest branches down, then my sister Susan, John and myself drag the branches down the fields back to the cottage where John and my mother would chop them up for the fire. In winter all the fields lay silent under the spell of nature. The birds stop singing and all the little creatures go to ground. The children's fingers are stiff and numb as they drag their branches, and they feel as if they are walking on air, their minds elevated by the cold. They feel as if they are not part of the world which lies like a flat white saucer at their feet, before them.

Susan, Anna and John with Judy the dog

Susan in the cold snow in the fields above the cottage

Carn Symphony

The trees continue to crackle and creak
The wind to rush and whine
The crows continue to cackle and speak
In a language lost in time.

Still the wind blows harshly across the cold land, the hedges shiver and all the ponds near the Wishing Well are frozen. There is ice on all the puddles. The village children come walking to collect firewood too. They crack the ice with sticks and bring old prams to put the firewood in. Their fingers too, are blue with the cold. They swing their arms to try to keep warm.

Back in the fields, the crows and the seagulls seem to laugh at our attempts to drag the branches down to the cottage. Being the smallest I was always bringing up the rear, dawdling, dreaming and grappling with my allocated branch, which was always much bigger and heavier than me. And all the while we were surrounded by the cold bay.

When we arrived back at the cottage, cold and tired John would chop up the branches into logs and our mother would light the fire.

Then the best time of day would be with us when the fire was lit and the kettle of water was placed on the logs. We would all huddle around the fire and a ring of backs would shut out the bleak Cornish day. Then the old kettle, burnt black from years of fire and flames would sing and splutter and the tea would be made. This always tasted of sweet burnt wood smoke. But it was good to hold a hot mug and to be sat in front of the warm fire. We children sat and gazed into the fire. Often we listened to the radio, 'Lord of the Rings' by Tolkien, was serialized for Children's Hour on Radio Four, and we could listen to the story whilst staring into the fire, imagining the faces and the places in the tale. Insects would emerge from the logs and scuttle to the safety of the chimney.

As the flames curled around the damp silver birch, the sap would ooze and spit. The cottage was impossible to heat as draughts blew in from everywhere: through the ill fitted windows, through the broken door, through the broken pane of the skylight and under the very rafters crept the Cornish gales.

Our mother pinned up an old army blanket across the partition, but with each gust of wind the blanket would billow, the wind would be sucked up through the massive red brick fireplace to return back down into the room bringing with it clouds of smoke from the fire.

Wild driving rain and roaring winds would rage about the cottage like mad monsters trying to get us children, trying to find some weak spot to break through.

The Smugglers

If you listen carefully
You will hear
How the gale lifts
The latchkey door my dear
And how the wind
Blows in from the cliffs
And shouts for more

And then the wind increases
to a mighty roar
and all the senses cease
to hold the body
once more

The elements so powerful
could end it all for us
and in one swift reappraisal
be gone before to dust

The wind blows
from the cliffs
the latchkey lifts
in the cottage
by the sea
the timbers creak
the roof leaks

yet all
is as should be

And in your dreams
you startle
and jump
to be amazed
the ring of darkness sparkles
and in this sleepy haze
the sound of horses
clashing
on the granite cold
you hear the smugglers laughing
then the masters voice scold.

And peeping through
the window
you see the lantern blaze
as down to the seashore
the smugglers make their way

Then in the distance
you see
the vessel in distress
the waves dancing madly
in their white ballroom dress
and as the evil spider
lures the fly
to its doom
the candle light flickers
in your cosy bedroom.

The ship is dashed to pieces
against the cruel rocks
in vain the crew
is heard to cry
while the wind
roars and mocks
No one can save the crew now
the smugglers maliciously jeer
tonight we will have our fill
of jewels and food and beer

Again the candle flickers
the cat stirs
on your bed
you lie back down
to sleep
to rest your weary head
And in the morning waking
you wonder 'if 'twas a dream
and rush to the casement
to see what can be seen
And down below the rocks
you see a terrible sight
bodies floating face down
that reaffirms the night.

XI: MADRON CHAPEL

Life was so hard for our mother. always wondering where our next meal was coming from and always keeping a brave face for us children. Despite this, she was fastidious in our grooming and our appearance. On sunny Sunday mornings she would wash our clothes outside the cottage door. She would stand in front of a rickety old wooden table on which was placed a plastic bowl. At the side of the bowl would be a large green block of Fairy washing soap, and while she washed our clothes she would listen to Desert Island Discs on Radio 4. Still today the theme music from this programme transports me back to that cottage door. For a short while this was Marjorie's way of shaking the cares from her shoulders and releasing the claws of war which had dug in deeply. She had the sun and the air on her cheeks as she washed away her troubles. She loved the sense of freedom it gave her.

The war had started on her sixteenth birthday and had ended when she was twenty one. And glancing down the fields, to the beautiful bay and St. Michael's Mount, Marjorie would remember the days of the bombings and the seemingly endless nights spent sheltering in the dark cellar. And although she could not give her children toys or material possessions, she could give them freedom of the soul and the chance to run through the golden grasses to where their little legs could carry them. She did her very best for us and every Sunday afternoon we would attend the little Methodist Sunday School at Madron Chapel. All morning our mum would work to get us children clean and tidy. Our hair was brushed and styled immaculately and our teeth and nails impeccably brushed. Our clothes were clean and ironed and Marjorie would even have saved some pennies for us to put in the collection. No one guessed that we lived in a granite cottage that was little more than a barn. We children loved our mother with the unquestioning innocence of childhood, we did not know then of her pain or sacrifice.

Anna, Susan and John ready for Sunday school

Then we would set off to walk the two miles to Madron Chapel. Sometimes we would be lucky enough to have bikes to ride. In summer the fields were full of wild flowers and the sweet smell of tansy would escort us, the lanes were full of blossoms and the heady scent of the elderflower and hawthorn. We learnt to grow strong in spirit, just as our mother had done when she was a child.

The little Sunday School at Madron Methodist Chapel was then run by two amazing nurses, Nurse Goldstone and Nurse Toms. The village of Madron was blessed when these two ladies came to work for Madron and the surrounding area in 1957. As well as all their district nursing they also delivered all the babies in the village.

Madron was very lucky to have these wonderful ladies who did such caring and compassionate work for their community. The Nurses also ran a Youth Club at the Chapel and a Summer School. We will never know the full extent of all their kind work and deeds as they were far too humble to tell us all that they did.

Attending the Sunday School was similar to a form of meditation. You could forget your worries for a couple of hours and just be happy, sing and learn to appreciate and care about each other.

Madron Methodist Chapel, was built in 1902, and is situated in Fore Street, just up the hill from the King William IV pub, on the left hand side.

Three original mallets, which were used to lay the cornerstones of the Chapel, are still kept in the village. The original Wesleyan Chapel was founded in 1800 and was built on the other side of the road directly opposite the new Chapel. Rose Matthews can remember playing in the ruins of this Chapel as a little girl. In those days there were no cars so it was safe for the children to play in the streets. Rose said they would play hopscotch, tops and whips and ball games. The tops were wooden and they would compete to see who could decorate their tops in the most colorful designs. If their ball went over the walls of the chapel they would climb in to retrieve it and stay to play in the ruins. Rose can remember that the walls were made of thick granite blocks. Rose had a lot of companions to play with as her mother, Annie Laura Matthews, had fifteen children.

In the early twentieth century the gap between the social classes was very marked. This divide was reflected in the attendance at the Churches and Chapels.

The farm owners and land owners attended Church, while those who worked on the sea and in the mines and fields were inclined to attend the chapels.

These workers felt that the Methodist Chapels were more sympathetic to their way of life. As children we were sent to the Methodist Chapel. Methodism was strong in its basic approach. The congregation celebrated the richness of the land as illustrated in the beautiful Harvest Festival Hymn which begins 'We plough the fields and scatter'. This embodies the ethos and the work ethic of the time.

When John Wesley first came to preach Methodism in the late 18th century, he did in fact come down to Cornwall to preach in St. Just and also at the Baptistery at the Madron Wishing Well.

Surprisingly, John and Charles Wesley were Anglican Priests. The object of Methodism was to evangelise, not to replace or compete with the Anglican system.

110

XII: MADRON CHURCH, MADRON SCHOOL AND TRENGWAINTON

Madron Church and Madron School nestle side by side on the top of the hillside, just like the mother doe and her baby fawn. The church tower can be seen from the surrounding countryside, standing majestically on the pinnacle of Madron Hill.

Richard the Lionheart, (Richard I), was born on 8th September, 1157. It is recorded that in the time of Richard the Lionheart, who was King from 6th July, 1189 until his death on the 6th April 1199, Henry de Pomeraye built and endowed the church at St. Madron, and gave it to the Knights Hospitallers of St. John of Jerusalem. Of the church which Henry de Pomeraye built only the font remains, which is Norman

The present church consists of a nave and chancel, with North and South aisles and a tower at the West end of the Nave. The two lower stages of the tower and the East end of the chancel (the ancient sanctuary) are much older than any other portions of the building, and form parts of the church which was rebuilt on the site of Pomeraye's church in the beginning of the 14th century.

Madron Church was the first village Church to ring out its bells when the 'HMS Beagle' and the dispatch boat 'Pickle' brought the sad news of the death of Lord Nelson, to the shores of Penzance, on 21ˢᵗ October 1805. Lord Nelson had been victorious in the battle of Trafalgar but had paid the ultimate price.

If you enter the churchyard up the steps from the village green, and stand to the right on the elevated grass, you can in fact look into the little classrooms of the school. It was in that end classroom, which was then Mr. Monk's class, that on cold blustery rainy winter mornings we would stand in the warmth of the open stove and sing one of my favourite hymns "For Those in Peril on the Sea". And as we sang we would look through the tall classroom windows as the harsh winds blew around the gravestones and the grass, while the flames from the open stove sent out a comforting glow. We sang with the courage and conviction of the innocent, with the world swirling and growing all around us.

Anna in a school play at Landithy Hall, Madron

I was six years old when I started at Madron Daniel's School, as the school was known then. Madron Daniel School was endowed through the kind generosity of George Daniel for the children of Madron.

It was a shock for me on my first day at school as it is for most children. For six years all I had known was the company of my Mother, brother and sister and the old cottage, the fields and the carn. On that first day at eleven o'clock when it was time for milk I decided that I had had enough and was going home. I can remember putting on my coat and woolen bonnet and running out of the school gates. As I got half way up the Village Green I glanced behind me to see the School Head Master, Mister Monk with a bright red face, tweed jacket and tie flapping in the wind, running up behind me. He apprehended me in a kind manner, and returned me to the fold.

However there were other first day saboteurs plotting mayhem as well as I. Not long after my return a new boy knocked over the water tray and us children all had to sit on the desks whilst the flood was mopped up.

When all was calm we returned to our desks and I tied my leg with my scarf, to the desk where my brother John was sitting and refused to move. My brother John is only one year and ten months older than me.

And so in the little school next to Madron Church, John and I, and later on, our little sister Cathy spent our early days.

On cold winter mornings we would awaken in our little cottage in the Dale to the sound of torrential rain, and gale force winds beating on the white washed slate tiles above our heads. If we were lucky the farmer's wife would give us a lift down to the Wishing Well corner where we could catch the bus to school. Failing that we would have to struggle in the rain against the gales, up the bank that led towards Ding Dong mine to catch the bus from there. We then had to wear old macs over our heads and shoulders to try to keep dry. Where the bank met the road was an old sign post which said 'Ding Dong', and pointed toward the mine. The actual sign has long gone and a new one has replaced it saying 'Bosiliac'. It was here that we hid our old macs in the bushes before catching the green double decker bus to school.

When the weather was fine we children enjoyed the trip up the bank to catch the bus to school. The whole world seemed transformed on those days. We walked with the spirits of our ancestors on the same path that the cavemen and the Iron Age Settlers had walked, as they hunted, lived and explored the wild land. The path we took from Boswarthen up to the Ding Dong bus stop has now completely grown over. Gorse bushes have grown to conspire with hawthorn trees, brambles have rambled to entwine ferns and moss, those granite stones that we knew so well have been completely covered. Yet can the voices of little children still be heard, when the cold North wind ceases to blow from across the moors, and the first cuckoo of spring calls?

There were only three classrooms then in the school at Madron: the infants, the middle class and the top class. The top class was Mr. Monk's, the Headmaster.The middle class was Mrs Cooper's and the infants, Miss Simmons.

We had little equipment in the classroom but we did have a radio and we all loved to join in with 'Singing Together', to learn old English Folk songs and sea shanties. We learnt such songs as 'Hearts of Oak', 'Jennie Jenkins' and 'The British Grenadiers'.

The Head Master was always immaculately dressed and smoked a pipe. He smelt of tobacco and Old Spice aftershave. On Monday mornings when we were in his class we had nail inspection. We all had to stand by our desks with our hands held out in front. The Headmaster would solemnly parade around the sniffling, snuffling, shuffling troops looking for anything untoward. There were also regular visits from the nit nurse. This would be either Nurse Toms or Nurse Goldstone, the nurses who lived next to the school in their purpose built house. The nurse would arrive and disappear into the headmaster's office with her unguents and her combs and each child would be ceremoniously called in for the head inspection

John and I often walked home from Madron School so that we could save our three pennies which would have been our bus fare. A lady we called 'Aunty Edmonds' who wasn't our real aunty lived at 'Far End', one of the last cottages in the village next to Parc Abnac, just before you walked across the fields to Boswarthen.

Aunty Edmonds and her husband Charlie were good friends of my mothers, and became God parents to John and Susan. Often on school days as we began our weary walk home we would be passing by 'Far End' and they would invite us in. Waiting for us on a large old oak table there would be freshly baked ginger bread and homemade-lemonade.

Aunty Edmonds would recall the days of her youth when she had worked at Trengwainton House in Madron. This beautiful old medieval house was acquired in 1867 by Thomas Simon Bolitho. It was left to Lieutenant Colonel Edward Bolitho in 1925, and with the magnificent gardens was given by him in 1961 to the National Trust, with provision for the family to live there. Aunty Edmonds was employed at Trengwainton House as a maid in the early 1900's when she was a girl. When balls and parties were imminent at the house there was great bustling and excitement.

When all her work was finished and the party was about to begin, Aunty Edmonds and several of the other maids would hide behind the banisters on the landing, where they had a view of the proceedings. They would peep through the banisters to look through the windows. They watched as the coaches arrived for the party with their immaculate coachmen and the fine horses tossing their brushed manes. The coaches would circle around until it was time for each coach to be received. Then the glamorous guests would alight to be announced, each dressed in fine attire.

Trengwainton

Tiptoe down
Through the trees
Where royal rhododendron
stand
at ease

See the camellia
Serene and still
Across a pretty bridge
And magnificent magnolia
Blossom
Amongst the dark green foliage

Now to the lake
Where the coaches
Circle around
With ceremonial flair
and the scent of the flowers
and the blossoms
carousel
on the evening air

From their carriages
Step the ladies
With their jewels
Their feathers their fur
Top-hatted descend the Lords
With their canes
And their
Haute couture

Yet please spare a thought
For the scullery maids
Underneath those
Fading skies
As they peep
Through polished bannisters
With their tired
And pretty eyes

With a million lamps
The house is lit
Candles blaze bright
In the hall
Moths and music

twirl and flit
sweet notes
and silk dresses swirl
Oh! Those golden memories
Of when Aunty was only a girl

And so our infant schooldays passed in an entanglement of rainy mornings and sunny walks home, across the granite stiles and through the friendly fields. Visions of school clothes drying beside wood burning stoves: of first crushes, singing together and boys getting the cane. There would often be tears when things went wrong but teacher would make it right again. The profound words of Mr. Monk I still remember today. He would ask the class which were the two saddest words in the English dictionary. The class would all chant in unison 'too late'.

Marjorie, Anna, John and Susan on the beach after school

XIII: MADRON WORKHOUSE

How we whirl, cascade, tumble
and weave our intricacies of life,
but God and the poor
the Wishing Well and the crows
remain the same

Often on sunny days we would walk to the village of Madron from our little cottage tucked under the dale. On warm spring days the air would be heavy with the scented blossoms of the elderflower and the hawthorn, and in the soft lanes we walked along the tansy and moss were like cushions below our feet. My mother wore a silver broach which was embossed with a Viking Ship, on the left lapel of her coat, and I can remember wondering how long it would be before I was as tall as that ship. Then in the lane we would pass the old Celtic cross of granite and we children would dare each other to run around the cross seven times 'for then' the old folks said 'you would see the devil'.

At the end of the lane on the left hand side was an old granite slab about four feet high, on which the farmer would leave the milk churns which had been brought down from the farm with the horse and cart. I would wait in our cottage garden for the horse and cart to come trundling past. I must have been about four years old. The farm labourer would pick me up and place me on the cart with the milk churns, and I would ride down to the Wishing Well and back. The name of the farm labourer was Leonard, and he would call me 'Miss What', as that is all I ever answered to his questions. The milk lorry would then pick up the churns that Leonard had left on the granite slab. I would then ride back to the hamlet of Boswarthen with Leonard on the horse and cart. Just past the granite slab where the milk churns were left, is a narrow hawthorn covered track that still leads to the Wishing Well and the Celtic Baptistery.

As my mother and I continued our walk, in front of us was then a stile which led to three fields and was a short cut to the village of Madron. On rainy days these fields were too muddy to cross so we would have to walk around the road way. Once in the fields the silhouette of the workhouse would come into view. The outline of the house was strange and foreboding: its dark towers rising like some horror house against the sky. The building looked South across the village of Madron towards Mounts Bay.

Mother would tell us the story of the Workhouse and from then on the building always seemed to have dark clouds above it, and we would hold her hand a little tighter thinking of the little ones who were not as lucky as us.

In the 1800's low prices of copper and tin in England forced a lot of men to find work overseas. The men left Cornwall and emigrated to Australia, America and Canada. They left behind their wives and children to exist in the Workhouse with the hope that they would return. The majority of these men never returned. They left behind their families, forever institutionalized in the Workhouse, where they lost all hope for the future.

When the children of the workhouse were admitted their old clothes were burnt and they were given a dark brown serge uniform to wear. The girls were given brown dresses and the boys brown trousers and shirts. On the children's shoulders were embroidered the initials MP, to signify Madron Poor. Both boys and girls were given hobnail boots to wear. On Sundays they would be marched down Fore Street, the sounds of their boots echoing through the village. They attended the Sunday School at the church which helped to fund the workhouse.

Records of Madron Workhouse actually go back to 1757. Then, there were large green gates at the entrance, and high walled gardens where the residents grew vegetables. There was also a field where they kept pigs and cows and chickens.

The residents also did laundry and ironing in the Workhouse. Parc Abnac Estate as it is known now was once a lane bordered by allotments also belonging to the Workhouse.

In 1838 a new building was erected. This was built during the time of the Napoleonic Wars (1790 - 1815) and was built by the prisoners of war. The prisoners were allowed to live there when they had finished the building.

Vida Matthews, who lives in Madron can remember delivering bread each day to the Workhouse, when she was a young girl of nine years old. She would collect the bread from Mrs. Cock at the village shop. She would carry six large loaves of bread in a huge wicker basket. On arrival at the big gates she would have to declare her business to the Gatekeeper, who would then let her through to walk up the lane to the house, so that she could deliver the bread to the Master of the Workhouse. He would then pay her a brass threepenny bit. Vida would then take the threepenny bit straight back to Mrs. Cocks' shop to buy two bread splits, a penny oxo and a penny's worth of humbugs. Mary Cock, the daughter-in-law of Agnes Cock who ran the village shop on the corner of Fore Street and Aldreath Road, can remember that the bread was kept in a large wooden box on the floor next to a large drum of paraffin. There was no such thing as Health and Safety in those days

The Master of the Workhouse was also known as 'The Beadle', and was employed to oversee the residents of the workhouse and keep them in order.

'The Beadle' was impressively dressed in a scarlet red jacket with brass buttons and white trousers. He must have seemed very frightening and intimidating to the children, who due to lack of food and heat were often sent to bed at four 0' clock in the afternoon.

The workhouse did continue into the twentieth century, even though the occupants were indignant about their situation. Yet the children were all eager to learn, and were accepted kindly by the village children. Residents of Madron can remember being at school with the children in the 1940's.

Humiliation was experienced by husbands and wives as they were separated into different wings of the house.

A very good friend of my mother's recalled a story of an old couple who met this same fate. The couple were in their eighties. The husband fell ill and the old lady was too frail to look after him. The authorities put them in the Workhouse and separated them.

Every morning the wife would totter down to meet her husband. They would hold hands and discuss their plans for one day returning to their little house. After sixty years of being together all they had left were a few humble possessions which they had managed to bring with them. In the evenings they would kiss goodnight and go their separate ways. Sadly, they both died in the workhouse and this is my little tribute to their love, on the next page.

Goodnight My Darling Bessie

When we return
to our cottage by the sea
how good
our lucky lives will be
you shall have
fine dresses of silk
fine puddings to eat
and sweets and milk

When we return
to our cottage by the sea
you shall have
fine clothes and hats
no more gruel
or cold
or rats

now sleep
my darling Bessie
the night grows
cold and damp
the evening star
is twinkling
and the Beadle
brings his lamp

And all the stars
in heaven
shine brightly
just for you
the moon
has shown
his friendly face
and sends
his love down too

In 1970, on November 19th, the foreboding dark building which had been the isolation block was pulled down. The isolation block of the workhouse had seen many types of ailments including scarlet fever, tuberculosis and other infectious diseases. One can imagine the sadness and the sorrow contained in that building. I live in Madron today and I am convinced that at certain times of the day , the small dark black clouds, that arise from that area of Madron are a residue of the dark despairing thoughts of the inhabitants of the workhouse.

The children of the village would play in the ruins and the empty workhouse. The old building was tumbling down and this cast a morbid fascination on us children. I once went in with one of my friends from Madron School. As we entered the derelict building my senses switched to overload. There was a smell of desolation emanating from the walls and the floors. The spirits of the sad and lonely seemed to swirl around us. The rooms were damp and musty with fungi and mildew growing on the walls. Underneath the house there were dark cellars and cells. Cold granite steps led down to these quarters. On the walls of the cells the prisoners had etched their names and these still remained to catalogue the fate of these unlucky individuals.

And so we children played in the abandoned workhouse, running apprehensively down the cellar steps wanting and not wanting some strange goblin type creature to jump from the dark recesses., and tell us in a high cackling voice that we were to be taken to that place where all naughty children had to go. We ran up the rickety wooden staircases into the bedrooms and the attic, or down the old wrought iron fire escape that was rusty and hanging off the wall on the outside of the building. In one of the attics I can remember finding old leather suitcases full of postcards and letters. These had stamps from all over the world on them and there were also letters to loved ones which had never been posted. After all these years a sinister question occurred to me. Why were all these letters and postcards, which were addressed to so many different people, all in one pile? The sinister answer came back. They probably never reached their true destination. It seems possible that the mail was intercepted by the overseers. The correspondence was from the men working in Australia and Canada, and the subsequent replies from their wives and children. If the overseers had given the mail to the families, the workers may have been able to leave the workhouse, and the labour force would have been depleted.

Many misfortunate people ended their days in the workhouse. Some of these characters had led reckless lives, some had suffered adversity, and some ill health and through no fault of their own, had ended their days in the workhouse.

Alfred Wallis, the mariner and painter of primitive sea scapes and ships lived there in the last years of his life. When he could no longer cope on his own in his little cottage in St.Ives he moved to the Workhouse in Madron. He was loved by the local residents of Madron who admired him for his sweet eccentricities. Mary Laity whose Grandfather worked at the workhouse, can remember Alfred Wallis walking down to the village shop, which was then run by Agnes Cock. He would ask for any old pieces of cardboard to do his paintings on. Alfred actually gave Mary some of his paintings, but when Mary's grandfather died these were thrown down Ding Dong mine shaft. Mary's aunty, Polly Tucker was a nurse at the Workhouse and Mary recalls that she spent a night there in the children's dormitory. The children had truckle beds. These had railings along the sides and the bedheads were made of iron.

Mary remembers that every Christmas they had a huge Christmas tree and that the choir from the Chapel and the Church would come and sing Carols. Mary also said that the garden was beautiful with all the flowers and vegetables grown there. The garden was surrounded by high granite walls and so was very sheltered. Mary still dreams that she is playing in the garden sometimes running in the grass and always surrounded by the high walls.

Sven Berlin, the sculptor, painter and writer, lived in Cornwall from 1938 until 1953. He befriended Alfred Wallis, and visited him in the workhouse. In Sven Berlin's book 'The Coat of Many Colours', he writes about Madron Workhouse.

* "So they had left their useless bodies lined up in a row of iron beds in a room painted green and brown, that looked out on a hill covered with rhododendrons"

This hill of course, was Madron Carn. The following poem is an extract from Sven's 'Coat of Many Colours'. He dedicated his book to the unknown artist.

"He who wears this coat puts on
The honour of the law of light
And shines as if a habergeon
Of silver blinds our sight

He is Knight of the butterflies
Warrior of the setting sun
Sinks as he lifts his head and dies
Blazing like a holy one"

*Extracts: Sven Berlin 'Coat of Many Colours' © 1994: Reprinted by permission for the estate of Sven Berlin www.svenberlin.com

These two painters must have had a brotherly affinity, both experiencing great hardships and austerity, despite the fact that there were fifty six years between them.   Alfred Wallis was born in Devonport on August 18th in 1855, and Sven was born in Sydenham, on 14th September 1911. Sven moved to Cornwall in 1938. He was an extremely gifted and talented sculptor, writer, poet and artist. Alfred did not start painting until he was 70 years old. Alfred painted with children's paints on any material which came to hand. Just like us children, he had to learn to improvise.

The Improvisers

My poem for Alfred;

And did the soft caterpillar realise
He would always have to improvise
When could he be 'Knight' and rise
To join the other 'butterflies?'

We children and Alfred
Experienced the same
*A go-cart buggy
From an old pram frame
A precious dolly
From a log of wood
A gifted painter
Misunderstood

---

* Our mother could not afford to buy John football boots, so she turned a blind eye when he dismantled my dolls pram to make a go-cart buggy, and cut up my Snow White dressing up dress, to make a Dick Turpin mask,

A sketch of the sea
On a cardboard box
One eye on the mast
One eye on the docks

My baby sister sleeps
In a dolly's pram
Mothers at the round table
Making tarts of jam

*A Dick Turpin mask
From a velvet frock
A sketch of a fish
On a granite rock

Now Alfred's hair is long and white
His beard is turning grey
He'll soon return to his childhood home
He'll see them all one day

The wind blows through
The hawthorn bushes
Rhododendrons bloom bright
On the carn
Alfred sleeps in his wrought iron bed
His sea a peaceful calm

Alfred Wallis died in Madron Workhouse on 29th August 1942, when he was 87 years old. His grave in Porthmeor Cemetery is a raised slab, the tiles were made by Bernard Leach. The inscription reads 'Alfred Wallis Artist and Mariner'.

In 1953 Sven left Cornwall and moved to the New Forest. There he wrote 'His Dark Monarch', his recollection of his St. Ives days.

Fragments

My poem for Sven;

Fragmentations of reality

Chip chip

The fragments fly

Desperate

To see the whole picture

But this world is just a lie

In his coat of many colours

Chip chip

The fragments fly

Misunderstood and starving

For this world

Is just a lie

Chisel, pen, pencil or brush
Chip chip
The fragments fly
Choose your weapons wisely
For this world
Is just a lie

In egocentric circles
The accusations fly
Hypocrisies
Confusion
For this world
Is just a lie

Sven Berlin died in Wimborne, Dorset on 14th December, 1999. I hope Alfred and Sven have lots to eat and drink now, and I know they blaze like holy ones.

XIV: THE BLUE SATIN DANCE DRESS

Time did sometimes seem to stop in the old granite cottage. Those were the days of early spring when golden sun beams shone down through the broken skylight window of the cottage, sending a million particles of sparkling dust, to dance down tunnels of time. They were the days when there was not a breath of wind in the fields and no creature great or small dared to break the silence.

Only the clock, next to the shiny brass bell, on the polished wooden bureau, was allowed to tick.

The golden day is silent. The old wooden stairs with thread-bare carpet, take you to the bedroom. The Spartan bedroom. No trappings, no decoration, no ornaments. Just an old double bed, under a massive, bulging chimney breast. There was a leak above the chimney in the eaves, which was plugged with an old rag. This was where my Mother slept, and gave birth to us children.

At the side of the bed, was an old wooden trunk. The trunk was full of a motley mixture of old clothes, dressing-up clothes. Here was an escape-route to a world of dreams and fantasies. In a small box at the bottom of the trunk, was an old brown felt hat with a feather at the side. Then there was a yellow and green satin cape with a high quilted collar, which could turn you in to a Persian King. Then there was a red velvet dress with puffed sleeves and a black velvet bodice, in which you could be Snow White.

Then there was the blue satin dance dress. Marjorie had loved to dance. Before the war Marjorie and Arthur would go to all the dances in Stockport, and dance to the music of the big bands. When a song came on the radio that reminded Marjorie of those days we would dance together, in front of the open fire. She taught me how to Waltz and Fox Trot. Marjorie had kept the dress as a reminder of those days, secretly hoping that one day she would wear it again.

As a child I would put on the dress and dance around the little bedroom. I imagined I was my mother dancing with my father before the war.

I would tiptoe up the narrow stairs with the threadbare carpet to the shelf that was the bedroom. The smell of the dust, the whitewashed granite and the vast expanse of time would pervade my nostrils. Now I dance with the man of my dreams and we are lost in a swirling tumbling dance of time. A man holds the door open for my mother to dance through, her eyes sparkle and the moonlight dances on her skin. His strong arms surround her and she is safe. Then the dream vanishes as my father dances away with his sheep skin coat, and his fat cigar.

I tiptoe to the banister and look over. Down below in the kitchen area there stands my mother. The loyal soldier who never deserts her post however hard the fighting becomes. She wears a cotton skirt she has made herself, each stitch a painful reminder of her loneliness. I wonder if she thought of the days, when all her clothes were made for her by her tailoress, Bessie Bleasby, and the dreams her proud father and mother had for her. Now she is my universe amongst the potatoes, the cauliflower, the crows calling from the carn, the cows in the field and the water from the well.

Now the army blanket billows when the gales blow, we children need new shoes and the skylight window leaks.

Once my mother danced in a blue satin dance dress. She carried a diamante purse that held a hanky and a lipstick. Now she carries buckets of water from the well.

Marjorie Aged 18 Years

135

I descend the stairs and call out 'Mum', she turns towards me with her soft brown hair tied gently back and her rainbow aura.

Marjorie was soft and gentle but she also had retained her pioneering spirit. Somehow we acquired an old television in a wooden frame.

The television was about to give up the ghost anyway, apparently the 'tube' had gone, and that was the reason that the picture rolled around the screen, and someone had to climb onto a chair with the aerial in order to achieve a clear picture. We children would argue about which programmes we wanted to watch. Marjorie threatened us saying that if we didn't stop arguing she would chop the television up. We didn't stop arguing so she did chop the television up. She took the axe and the offending box up on to the field in front of the cottage and kept her word. She did us children a favour, because then we had to listen to the radio and use our imaginations in life.

With all the struggle and the loneliness my Mother became tired of being on her own. The days were long and the nights even longer, for days and days she only had us children to talk to. She must have longed for company. She decided to go for a drink in the pub at Madron. She became friends with some of the parents at Madron School and sometimes they would come back to the cottage with guitars, and it was good to hear our mum enjoying herself with laughter and song. Then she met a man and began an affair and our lives changed drastically again.

Sometimes he would come up to the cottage to see her, and yet again we would sit in our little window seat and watch as this tall dark figure came striding up the lanes towards the cottage.

Then one evening he called and my mother would not let him in.

He had been drinking and had brought lots of bottles of beer with him. He desperately started banging on the old wooden door with the bottles and my mother dragged a large tin trunk behind the door to stop him breaking in. He tried and tried to get in and us children lay shivering in our beds as we heard bottles being smashed against the door.

Eventually he gave up and all was silent. It was not long after this incident that we learnt that our mother was to have another child. We had nothing. How were we going to cope?

138

XV: CATHY IS BORN

On the evening of 10th June 1962 there was disharmony in the cottage.

The Elsan toilet at the bottom of the garden needed emptying. Usually our mother would dig a hole in the field next to the cottage and empty it herself but she was now eight months pregnant and she needed help.

The weather had been extremely hot. The heat waves rose above the potato fields in wavy lines. The earth was dry. Tractors drove down the lanes and clouds of dust followed them. Rain was needed.

The water in the tank outside the cottage was low. The children leaned over to look in. Slugs and snails and unrecognizable reptiles swarmed in the murky bottom. At best we could only boil and wash in the water. It was not fit to drink. Even the water in the well was low.

The potato picking had begun in the fields surrounding

the cottage. The farm hands and labourers returned from the fields with dusty black faces. Children from the village of Madron came up to pick potatoes. For us children it was an opportunity to make some pocket money.

Sue, John and I went potato picking so that we could save up our wages and go to the Corpus Christi Fair which came to Penzance every year. There was much excitement amongst us children when the fair eventually arrived. We would sit in the little bedroom window, and when the hot summer breeze was blowing in from the sea we could hear the music of the fair, even though it was three miles away. We could hear the whirl of the big wheel and the screams of the riders. It all seemed so mysterious and such great fun.

Potato picking was hard work. The tractor and trailer would leave the farm early in the morning. We would all jump on to the trailer and it would take us to the designated field for the day. The hot smell of the potatoes and the soil would be under our nose. We children would have to kneel in the soil to fill the heavy cast iron buckets full of potatoes, and then carry the buckets to the end of the row to empty them into the Hessian sacks. For this arduous task we children would receive one old shilling per 100 weight sack that we filled. The old farmer, Captain Ben, would follow us children behind. Raking the ground with his walking stick to make sure we did not miss any, he would shout "scrabble for em kids, scrabble"

We were all exhausted from working in the fields that day, but the toilet still needed emptying. Marjorie decided to do it herself. What else could she have done? She worked herself into such a state that she seemed to overlook the fact that she was eight months pregnant. She dug with the adrenalin of desperation. We children, huddled in the little window, watched as she carried the heavy Elsan and emptied it in the garden. We did not understand the seriousness of the situation. My mother even though so heavily pregnant had been potato picking as well as us children. She wore a long khaki mackintosh, wellingtons and a head scarf in the warm sun of that hot June day.

When evening fell and Marjorie's work was done there was nowhere for her to bathe, very little water and very little food.

The next morning at 6:43 a.m. on June 11th 1962 my sister Cathy was born.

We were awoken by the sound of our mother in labour. She lay giving birth under the massive white washed chimney breast, under the hole in the roof and the old rag that plugged the hole. She lay under the beams that tangled with the ivy that grew in from outside. The ivy that during the day hid the creepy crawlies that dropped on you in the night.

My sister Sue went across to Mum's bedroom to help and she could actually see the head of the baby about to be born. She ran across to the farm house, where they had the only phone in the hamlet, and asked the farmer's wife to phone the midwife. Audrey Thomas, the farmer's wife, then phoned and was told that there was no record of a baby being due in Boswarthen. It seems that Marjorie's pregnancy was not registered with the midwives. This however may have been a blessing in disguise, as this was the sixties when lots of pregnant women were unwittingly prescribed thalidomide for morning sickness.

John and I were afraid and sat holding hands in our little

box window and glancing down the fields to the beautiful bay
in the golden morning sunshine we whispered to each other
"what do you want? a boy or a girl?" We felt lost as no one had
prepared us for the event.

When Sue returned to the cottage the baby was then
actually on the bed with the umbilical cord still attached. She
ran back yet again to the farmer's wife and shouted "'the baby
is on the bed" and the farmer's wife then came back with Sue,
and standing by the bed held my mother's hand. The hour of
absolute panic and fear that Sue had experienced from the time
of her being awakened at five o'clock, completely dissolved
into relief, with the arrival of Nurse Goldstone the midwife
from Madron. The midwife's dark blue gabardine uniform
and her gentle kind ways reassured Sue, who at one stage had
even thought that mother was going to die.

Then the farmer's wife took John and I across to the
farmhouse where we sat in the warm kitchen. The stove had
been lit and the large kitchen table had been set with what
seemed to us a massive breakfast feast. There was bread and
butter, cold meats and preserves, jam marmalade and fruit and
most amazingly of all to us children at breakfast time, fancy
cakes. We sat as quiet as 'two blind mice', as the farmer's
wife held a large loaf of bread against her chest. It was as if
she had the bread in a headlock and was trying to strangle it
with one arm, whilst she sliced across it towards herself with
the other. She did in fact have a large carving knife. Then the
hungry farmer returned from the milking parlour where he
had started work at 4am. We sat and watched as he devoured
bacon and eggs followed by buns and fairy cakes. And the
early morning slid into the day. As we sat in the kitchen in
total bewilderment and wonder, a new life was emerging in

our humble cottage across the lane.

Nurse Catherine Goldstone had in fact arrived at 6:45 a.m. just two minutes after the baby was born at 6:43 a.m. Sister Sue and Audrey Thomas, the farmer's wife had done a good job. My mother called her baby Catherine after the kind mid wife.

Cathy was six weeks premature and weighed five and a half pounds at birth. The nurse weighed her in a terry toweling nappy. Cathy had to sleep in my doll's pram as we had no cot for her. I peeped into my doll's pram and there lay a real life baby with soft downy shoulders.

After the birth, my Mother was very poorly and Cathy cried a lot. My Mother had jaundice and my Sister Susan had to do a lot of hard work to keep the family together.

Sue had to take time off from school to look after Cathy, John and myself. As we had hardly any money and consequently little food it was a stressful time for us all. Yet we struggled on and Cathy grew into a beautiful little girl with light golden ringlets.

Cathy Aged 2 years outside the cottage

XVI: 'WHICH WAY IS THE WIND BLOWING?'

And as Cathy grew our stress turned into happiness. Now we had something positive to concentrate on, to help this small child grow and feel loved. We all adored Cathy, she was so cute. She quickly learned to improvise, and create her own toys. When she was still a toddler, she carried around a wooden log with a blanket wrapped around it, pretending it was a doll. Looking back this seems quite sad, the fact that our mother could not afford to buy toys. However, Alfred Wallis would have been proud of Cathy's improvising.

Simone (Susan and Michael Jordan's daughter) and Cathy

Gradually, as the days rolled by, our situation at the cottage started to improve. In 1963 Sue left school and was employed in Penzance Library. In 1966 John started work as an apprentice fitter at Holmans Dry Dock in Penzance. This meant that both Sue and John could now help Marjorie financially. John was able to attend Camborne Technical College on day release to study Technical Drawing.

Both John and Sue inherited Arthur's dynamic pragmatism. John became a clever engineer, also a gift inherited from his grandfather Miles, and he stayed to work in Penzance. Sue was also very inventive and now Sue had an income she was able to buy material and design and make her own clothes. The first dress I remember her making was in a soft mustard wool. It was a shift dress, and Sue wore it, as was the fashion of the time, with a black turtle neck jumper.

That Christmas a parcel arrived at the cottage from Arthur, in it there were Christmas jumpers for Cathy, John and I. These new clothes smelt unbelievable strange and wonderful, but the best present was the one Sue received. This was a shiny black box of Max Factor make-up, and perfume. Arthur was benefiting from the economic boom of the sixties as well. Sue acquired a tiny portable record player that played singles only, and she could now afford to buy records and we would push the furniture back and dance to the music of the 'Beatles, the Stones and the Searches'. We could ' Twist' and do the 'Hippy Shake Shake'. Cathy, who was still only a toddler would dance with us as well. On the whole the music scene then was uplifting and happy. The phoenix was rising. The spirit of the English peoples which had been squashed during the war was re-emerging. The austerity years of the fifties were almost at an end, and the carnival, led by Harold Wilson and the Beatles was beginning.

Harold Wilson was elected as Prime Minister on 15th October, 1964, and the Labour Party stayed in power until 18th June 1970. Harold Wilson achieved many social reforms in housing, health and education, during that time. There was certainly a new wavelength sweeping the land that carried with it an air of positivity that was the spirit of the decade.

The music and fashion scene was buzzing, in England. London was alive with the vibes of this new found freedom for entrepreneurial expression. Britain led the way in the Fashion world with designers such as Mary Quant, Zandra Rhodes, Ossie Clark, Bill Gibb and Jean Muir as the forerunners. On New Years Day 1964, Top of the Pops came to our television screen with happy songs and great excitement. It was certainly a privileged time to be young on this island.

In London the streets were the place to go, to show off your latest fashions, to see and be seen. Carnaby Street and the Kings Road were where the hip people hung out, and the Kinks sang about the 'Dedicated Follower of Fashion.' In Penzance several trendy boutiques opened, selling designer styled clothes, such as shift dresses, mini-skirts, culottes and white boots. For the lads there were slick suits, pink ties, and 'Beatle'.haircuts. For those who were fans of the 'Stones' there were flouncy shirts and velvet jackets a la 'Brian Jones' mode. The shops were all painted in the new Pop Art style, that made you feel as if you were on the set of an Alice in Wonderland film.

Meanwhile across the pond our brothers and sisters were caught in a terrible trap. It was the time of the Vietnamese War and the American involvement in that war. Running concurrently with the 'Flower-Power' movement which advocated 'Peace and Love', were the often violent clashes of the anti-war campaigners.

In London there were 'Ban the Bomb' peace rallies, and CND marches. While Tony Bennett crooned about visiting San Francisco and adorning your hair with flora and fauna. Lyndon B. Johnson, the then American President, insisted that "If we quit Vietnam tomorrow we'll be fighting in Hawaii, and next week we'll have to be fighting in San Francisco." As in the 1930s, so this was the treacherous undercurrent of the 1960's, waiting to burst its' banks at any minute. But in England we held it back, and thanks to Harold Wilson, British Troops were kept out of Vietnam. In America young lads were being sent to fight in a war which could have been avoided. There was compulsory conscription which fell mainly on to the youth of poor families, as those with money could extend their education, and stay at home. The conditions they had to fight in were similar to those experienced by the 'Chindits' in Burma. Often when the pressure got too much to bear, young lads would run screaming hysterically into the jungle to meet their waiting fate.

How can it be that the world seems so unfair? We had few possessions but we did not have war. Back in our little hamlet we were blessed with peace. Now we had actually acquired a record player. This was one of those that was in a box case. Now we could listen to the profound protest songs of Bob Dylan, 'The Times they are a changing', 'The Ballad of Hollis Brown' and 'Blowing in the Wind'. We would sit and listen to Dylans's powerful and spiritual voice, singing such songs as 'Masters of War' which was written in protest against the government, the military and the Cold War arms build-up of the 1960's. Dylan's voice melted into the granite, the fields and our psyche and seemed to embroider our own feelings we owned anyway of struggle, unfairness and survival in a world where the cards had been stacked against you. In Dale Cottage we were flower power hippies, we were against war and later marched with the CND.

Which way is the wind blowing?
Who knows? Who knows?
To which war are the young men going?
Who knows? Who knows?
The winds of war
Grow fierce and strong
And carry both good and evil along
Tyrants plot wars in their brand new suits
For money and for fame
Whilst young men die in their brand new boots
Only just pawns in their game

The anti-war movement of the 1960's, protested against the politicians, who created hatred between nations in order to start wars, and reap the rewards from the sale of arms.

In 1969, in America the 'Woodstock' festival was held. News had reached the public of America and England, of the terrible slaughter of the innocents in Vietnam. The American population was becoming increasingly angry at the situation. In 1969, the hippies of the nation banded together to show that they just wanted to live in peace. They wanted to stop the war. This culminated in three days of peace and music. It was held at Max Yasgur's 600 acre dairy farm in the Catskill mountains, in the town of Bethel, New York, from August 15 to 18th, 1969. Bethel is 43 miles southwest of the town of Woodstock, New York.

His Holiness Sri Swami Satchidananda, opened the festival. He is the founder of 'Integral Yoga' and has dedicated his life to peace both for the individual and the world. He opened the festival thus:

* "My Beloved Brothers and Sisters, I am overwhelmed with joy to see the entire youth of America gathered here in the name of the fine art of music. Music is a celestial sound and it is a sound that controls the whole universe, and with that sound, man will not become animal to kill his own brethren."

Many of the songs at the festival were sang by anti-Vietnam war protesters, such as Country Joe and the Fish, Joan Baez, Ravi Shankar and Richie Havens. Jimi Hendrix, Joe Cocker, Janis Joplin, Jefferson Airplane, among many others, sang as well, to an audience of over 400,000 people. After the event Joni Mitchell, who was not present at the festival, wrote the famous song, 'Woodstock'. This was taken from details of the festival that she had heard from her then boyfriend Graham Nash. This in its own gentle way was also a protest song against the Vietnamese war with allusions to 'the bombers', the peaceful 'child of God', and returning to the 'garden', the Garden of Eden.

I was still at school when this war was raging, and I can remember feeling really sad when hearing the news about the

---

*Sri Swami Satchidananda 1969, Woodstock Music Festival in Bethel, New York, August 15th, - Addressing a crowd of approximately 500,000 people. Quote used with permission from Satchidananda Ashram-Yogaville®/www.Yogaville.org

insane conflict. I would sit in the little granite window of the bedroom and write protest poems about the war. I couldn't believe what was happening, and that a whole generation of Americans had been affected by the conflict, but being a Capricorn and being ruled by the planet Saturn I was always melancholy and philosophical as a child anyway.

By this time Arthur had married his third wife and had taken a pub in Stockport called 'The Red Bull.' Soon Sue would leave Mum and the cottage to live with Arthur and his new wife Isobel, at the Red Bull. Sue then went to study Fashion and Design at Manchester University, in Manchester, otherwise known as the 'Toast Rack.' Sue still managed to send money down to help Mum.

Left to right: Marjorie, Susan, Simone, John and Anna. Happy days outside Dale Cottage.

151

John carried on working at Holman's Dry Dock as an apprentice. He was still helping our mother financially as well, and started to work on improvements to the cottage. He fixed things and mended things, painted, and did his very best for us all. Mum was able to buy seeds and grow flowers around the cottage for the first time. Even these small luxuries had been previously out of reach. John rode his bicycle to work in Penzance every day. In the morning he would awaken and shout to mum "which way is the wind blowing?" John had to 'clock on', for work at Holmans, and if the wind was blowing in from Mount's Bay, from the East, then it would delay him by about five minutes, and make him late.

John eventually bought a scooter, and bought a khaki army coat to wear for protection. The coat was very long and kept him dry from the rain. On his return from work, John would throw the door open and stand in the doorway in his long coat with his helmet on, looking like Darth Vader from Star Wars. Cathy was only four years old and would be frightened by John, and would run to hide behind the curtains. He always bought us sweets on pay day and gave me two shillings and sixpence pocket money. He would put his pay packet, which smelt of diesel oil and the sea, on top of the bureau so that mum could take what money she needed. Mum would bake plates of mince pies and jam tarts, which would be waiting on the round table for John's return. After tea we would all sit by the fire and talk and John would be smoking his Gold Leaf cigarettes which he had treated himself to with his wages.

John loved to dance as well. We had a massive old radio which lived in a recess next to the fire. John had to manipulate a strange wheel in order to tune in to radio stations. Eventually he would locate Radio Caroline. This was a ship which was broadcasting radio programmes and was situated off the coast of Cornwall. Then we could dance to 'Canned Heat…I'm on the Road again' and 'Deep Purple..Black Night'. Now we could listen to a broader range of Rock and Roll music as the Radio Caroline ship 'Mi-Amigo' rocked and rolled off the East coast of England, with a 50kw transmitter broadcasting to the British Isles and even to Europe. At last we could have fun.

On Forever

So we borrow
These bodies on loan
For a lifetime
But our spirits
Go on forever
And swiftly moving
Through portals of time
We skip
Cross the moors
And the heather

With wild hair flowing
And swift fairy feet
We will dance
To the tune
Of the fiddler's beat
And though trapped
In a time warp
Or lost at sea
Our souls will fly on
Through eternity

XVII: THE CREATIVE ENERGY OF CORNWALL

And while we were dancing to the 'Stones' and becoming philosophical with Dylan, the painters, potters, and poets, were busy all around us. A group of artists rose to prominence in the 1950's and 60's and curiously were all born at the start of the twentieth century. Roger Hilton and Sven Berlin were born in 1911. Sir Terry Frost and Bryan Wynter were born in 1915. Sydney Graham and Peter Lanyon were born in 1918, Patrick Heron was born in 1920, and Rose Hilton, in 1931. One important artist who was not born in this era was Alfred Wallis who was born in 1855. Sir Terry Frost and Sven Berlin had both been taken as prisoners of war. This they said had intensified and heightened their artistic senses and had made them more spiritually aware. These artists all loved Cornwall for its wild remoteness, its intensity of colour and its alchemy of life. Arthur Slater was also painting, sculpting and working in wood at the same time. He carved the front door for the Admiral Benbow, depicting Neptune, a mermaid, and dolphins.

Sydney Graham, a Scotsman and poet, moved from Glasgow to Cornwall in 1943. Later, He moved to St.Ives with his wife Nessie Dunsmuir, and soon became friends with the painters of the St.Ives School of art. He became well acquainted with Bryan Wynter, Peter Lanyon and Roger Hilton. He moved to Madron in 1967, where he lived until his death in 1986. He would frequent the local alehouse and there are many accounts of his story telling and impromptu poetry recitals. He often wrote poetry for his artist friends, these elegies included: 'The Voyages of Alfred Wallis', 'Dear Bryan' for Bryan Wynter, and 'The Thermal Stair' for Peter Lanyon. He also wrote the poem 'Lines on Roger Hiltons Watch'. Verse eight of this poem says:

"I am only a watch

And pray time hastes away.

I think I am running down."

"Watch and pray, time hastes away" is the inscription on the face of the clock on Madron Church tower. This clock was given to Madron by the Bolitho family in 1999.

Sydney Graham also became good friends with our good friend Trooper Eddy Strick, who fought in Burma and was one of the 'Chindits'. They both shared a love of the Cornish countryside. And for our good friend Trooper Eddy Strick, Sydney wrote the following poem

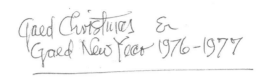

Gaed Christmas &
Gaed New Year 1976-1977

The cock may crow. The day may daw
An Eddy Strick has gaed awa.
He's gaed away for Christmas time
Tae meet his friends of another clime.
He's gaed awa tae Derbyshire.
Tae see Bobby Nichols a drink at the fire.

A guid Christmas tae Eddy Strick
An a guid Christmas tae Bobby Nichols.
A guid Christmas tae Bobby's wife
May ye a' have the time o' your life.
A Guid New Year tae the coos & sheep
And may the weather and God keep.

Eddy's gone up tae drink by the fire
Wae his chum in Derbyshire.

Sydney & Nessie
Madron

Edward John Strick: 3/12/1919 - 2/12/1996 'Gaed Christmas & Gaed New Year 1976
-1977' and extracts of the work by W.S.Graham in this publication, reproduced by
permission of Rosalind Mudaliar.
© The estate of W.S.Graham

157

And as the post-war painters painted in the style of abstract expressionism so the poets wrote in a similar vein. The writings of T.S. Eliot, Dylan Thomas and indeed Sydney Graham can be said to reflect the fragmentation of the society of the time, almost as if they are trying to piece back together their worlds which have been ripped apart. At other times their poetry seems surreal. Graham did in fact meet and work with both Eliot and Thomas in his early career. Sydney's poems are a mixture of contrasting emotions: profound yet homely; comforting and compassionate yet analytical. This can be seen particularly in his later collections of 'Malcolm Mooney's Land' (1970), and 'Implements in their Places' (1977). (Extract below)

"How pleased I am
To meet you reading and writing on damp paper
In the rain forest beside the Madron River."

One balmy summer's evening my friends and I did meet Sydney and his lovely wife Nessie. We did not have damp paper but we were barefoot and wrapped in colourful blankets like some lost Red Indian tribe. The day had been really hot and my sister Cathy and I and two friends hitch-hiked into Penzance to spend a peaceful day on the beach. On returning home we walked slowly, laughing and chatting, and as the evening air started to gently cool we turned our blankets into ponchos around our shoulders. As we walked through Madron, butterflies and moths flew around the bushes and flowers and the golden light of the setting sun shone from beyond the carn. We grew weary and tired and the souls of our feet became black with tramping through the dust.

Then like some ethereal cavalry coming over the hill, through the breathless evening air we heard the strains of a Beethoven Symphony. We could not tell from where the music was coming so we stopped and sat down to lean against a granite wall to rest and listen to the music. As we sat, tired but happy, a pretty head popped over the wall "My dears" exclaimed the bright lady, in a sweet Scottish accent "do come in and rest for a while". And so we entered the small granite cottage with Nessie, and there sitting at an old wooden table with a small white candle burning in the now fading light sat Sydney Graham. The table was covered with papers, pens, pencils, journals and books. We had found the source of the mystical music.

Even though we had disturbed Sydney's work he turned his chair and chatted to us. Nessie made us welcome and bought us tea and biscuits and Sydney, intrigued by our appearance, asked us all our names and ages.

So there we sat with the Scottish Sage and his lovely wife and laughed and chatted about how exquisite the hot day had been, and where we had been swimming.

My Poem for Sydney;

Captain

The Captain of the written word
raised his compound head
and reading from lines
he had just penned
softly and slowly
he read.

And there we sat together
in the gathering gloom
while Sydney's words
across the granite tumbled
into that rustic Cornish room
and as nostalgic notes
tiptoed on the cool night air
Sydney smiled
and turned on his chair
had we known what lay in store
could we have steered our ship to shore?

We thanked Nessie and Sydney for their kind hospitality and for letting us enter into their world. We left the little cottage feeling enriched from our meeting and revitalized by the refreshments. We walked the soft darkening lanes, and we crossed the fields of harvested corn, the stiff straws of corn piercing our feet. As the night started to draw its shadowy curtain across the land, we saw the foxes and badgers returning to their lairs. We sleepily returned to our little cottage under the dale, the sweet smell of the meadows lulling us into a sleep of babies, in our world of harmony and peace. And with the words of John Wesley we leave the sleeping souls in "the heavy slumber of humanity"

XVIII: 'AND IN THE END'

And as we leave those sleeping souls, I must leave you soon too. Thank you for travelling with me and sharing my journey. Once again I find myself at the cottage door, and as my story starts to close, my spirit returns to the place of my birth, and my past, my present, and my future are one.

And swirling, swirling
the earth keeps turning
while the clouds scud past
in soft array
and the Cornish sun
shines molten gold
and will shine
for us all
another day.

We cannot escape from the consequences of space and time, and the cycles of life.

And now I see her. She is dressed in a long brown felt coat that the farmer's mother-in-law has given her. A quite elegant coat. The waist is gathered in with neat pleats, then the soft brown material flounces out in a full skirt which reaches down to her calves. On the bodice at the front of the coat, are embroidered small flowers in brightly coloured silks, reflecting the hippy flower power ethos of the time. The few small moth holes on the hem of the coat only add to its charm. On her head she wears a hat that is also made of brown felt and has a wide brim. Her long golden brown hair falls from under her hat down to her waist. Her hair is sun-kissed and soft, washed in rainwater taken from the top of the murky tank. She wears old faded jeans that are patched with crochet squares that are cut from a blanket that her grandma had made, and sent down to the cottage. She knows no boundaries, no structure. From her past and the past of her ancestors she has inherited a restlessness of her soul.

In a small bag she carries her worldly belongings. She walks into her future, as I have walked into my past. She is seventeen and leaving home. The night before she had sat by the old red brick fire for the last time, with her mother, her sister and her brother. John had said "Don't go Anna". Now she realizes that the grass is not always greener on the other side. But we must all make our own mistakes and experiences. It is part of our individual karma.

Marjorie eventually moved back to Edgeley Stockport with Cathy, to live with her mother Emily, after the death of her father Miles. She lived happily in the comfort and safety of her childhood neighbourhood. She was at last able to enjoy the labour saving devices of the modern world. She had the luxury of things we now take for granted like taps and doors, things which she never had in Boswarthen. She died in 1995, on Cathy's birthday, June 11th when Cathy was just 33.

John stayed at the cottage for the longest of us all. On the 25th March 1971 he married Diane Klein and they lived together there until May 1976.

Then the cottage was empty and alone. The farmer used it for a wood store. The ivy started to grow back again from behind the chimney. When the Local Authority came to Boswarthen to assess buildings for listing, they passed it by, thinking it was just a barn. Yet the cottage was glad. It had time to mourn. It missed the family. It missed the children's laughter and the stories told beside its' massive red brick fire place. It was not ready to give up its' secrets. No one knew of the golden sunbeams that shone down through the broken skylight window, no one knew of the tears that the pretty little woman had shed as she polished the windows and swept the floors. And only the old cottage knew of the loneliness she had felt when the children were at school and she had only the cows to talk to. So the cottage drew the blanket of ivy around it and slept.

After Arthur's travels around Cornwall he also had returned to live in the North. He was living with brother John. It was as if both parents desired to return to be near their roots for safety, and to find that comfort blanket of their childhood. The ghosts of their family and friends resided in the red brick houses, that his brother Jim had left all those years previously.

There is a certain consolation in familiar surroundings, and both Marjorie and Arthur must have felt the need for the structural security of the 'dirty old town', where they were both born. Their wild days were spent, they had both come full circle, even if it was not together. The finishing post was the cobbled streets of their youth, the bakers' shops selling meat and potato pies, egg custards, vanilla slices and balm cakes. The scent of Robinsons Brewery on a wet wintry day, the sound of the cart horses hooves delivering the barrels on the dray. The rooftops of familiarity, and the faces of those who unpretentiously accept people for what they are, not who they aspire to be. The last time I saw my father was in Buxton, Derbyshire. That day Arthur and I said our goodbyes and hugged our last hug, as I was then leaving to live again in Cornwall. Arthur then started to ascend the stairs, and I to walk down the hall to the door. As I opened the door I turned to take one last look at Arthur, and being half way up the stairs, he with his hand on the stair rail, turned to look at me. He said nothing, he just smiled and winked, and then turned again to disappear up the stairs.

The last time I ever saw my mother was in a dream, just a week after she had died. Marjorie had been very ill with breast cancer and had lost a lot of weight. She appeared in the dream and had resumed her normal weight and was smiling. "Oh mum" I cried "You look so well", and we hugged. "I am well", she said, "it's great now, you can just think where you want to be and you are there", and then she laughed, "I've just had fish and chips with John." The next morning, still intrigued by the dream, I phoned up brother John, and told him the story. He laughed as well, he said that on the day before, he and his wife

Diane and their children had been to Falmouth for the day, and on the way back they had stopped to have a meal. Guess what was on the menu. Yes, fish and chips.

So it's a great relief to know that Marjorie is well, and I do hope she still thinks of Arthur and that she teleports to see him sometimes. Just to check he is all right. Maybe they could ride their tandem into the Derbyshire Hills again, and stopping on some windy hillside to eat sandwiches, they could talk about the old times and how they wished it had all worked out differently. They could read Chinese poems together, recite verses from Keats, and dream of a better world. Arthur could ask Marjorie to marry him again at St. Matthews Church in Edgeley. And if they're still hungry when they've had their sandwiches may be they could go for fish and chips.

And In The End

We walk on the beach
As the days have gone down
We talk of our youth
And the memories we own

We are children inside
But our skins have grown old
And like snails we glide
Shiny and cold

Each with their own story to tell
Each seeking protection
From their own shiny shell

Our memories we nurse
Our sorrows portrayed
Each suffered as children
In different ways
And the hurt has stayed with us
Down all the days

Yet the love is still there
And we learn to forgive
And to heal ourselves
We must love and let live

And the dandelions still grow
So beautiful and bright
As when we were babies
Innocent and right

And if we open our hearts
Then we too can shine
And the dandelions and snails
Will be there
For all time.

Au Revoir
Je Reviens
Anna

Bibliography

Huxley Aldous: - 'Ends and Means': Copyright © 1938 by Aldous Huxley. Reprinted by permission of Georges Borchardt, Inc., for the Estate of Aldous Huxley.

Churchill Winston: - 'The Gathering Storm: The Second World War, Volume 1' And quotation from Winston Churchill's Speech – 'We shall fight them on the beaches' Reproduced with permission of Curtis Brown, London on behalf of the Estate of Winston S. Churchill
Copyright © The Estate of Winston S. Churchill

Shakespeare William: 'Hamlet' - The Complete Works of William Shakespeare - Oxford University Press © 1910

Tolstoy Leo: 'War and Peace' - First Published © 1869

MacHorton Ian: 'Safer than a known way' In collaboration with Henry Maule
Publisher: Transworld Publishers Odhams Press Edition © 1958

Mosley Leonard: 'Gideon Goes to War'
Publisher: Arthur Barker; First Edition edition © (1955)

T.S Eliot: 'The Waste Land'
Publisher: New York: Boni and Liveright, © 1922

Fergusson Bernard: 'Beyond the Chindwin - Being an Account of the Adventures of Number Five Column of the Wingate Expedition Into Burma 1943'
Publisher: Collins London © 1945

"The rain it raineth on the just..." Quote by Charles Synge Christopher Bowen (1835–1896)

Websites

www.snowdoniasociety.org.uk

http://www.heretical.com/British/joyce.html

www.svenberlin.com